Unlucky Stiffs

Also by Cythnia Ceilán

Thinning the Herd: Tales of the Weirdly Departed

*Weirdly Beloved: Tales of Strange Bedfellows, Odd Couplings,
and Love Gone Bad*

Unlucky Stiffs

New Tales of the Weirdly Departed

CYNTHIA CEILAN

LYONS PRESS
Guilford, Connecticut
AN IMPRINT OF GLOBE PEQUOT PRESS

To buy books in quantity for corporate use
or incentives, call **(800) 962–0973,**
or e-mail **premiums@GlobePequot.com.**

Lyons Press is an imprint of Globe Pequot Press.

Layout artist: Kevin Mak
Project manager: Kristen Mellitt

Library of Congress Cataloging-in-Publication Data is available on file.

ISBN 978-1-59921-910-3

Printed in the United States of America

10 9 8 7 6 5 4 3 2 1

For **Tom.** I thought you were **dead.**

Table of Contents

Acknowledgments ix

Introduction xi

CHAPTER 1: The Best Laid Plans 1

CHAPTER 2: Dying for a Living 23

CHAPTER 3: Send in the Clowns 40

CHAPTER 4: Shoulda Stayed Home and
Ordered Chinese 54

CHAPTER 5: All Guts, No Glory 78

CHAPTER 6: Cured to Death 101

CHAPTER 7: I Love You to Pieces 121

CHAPTER 8: He Needed Killin' 142

CHAPTER 9: Gambling with the Rent Money 161

CHAPTER 10: Whiskey Tango Foxtrot 181

CHAPTER 11: Fun Facts about Death 211

Sources 236

About the Author 242

Acknowledgments

The life of a writer is solitary by necessity. That's what I like best about it.

Sometimes I poke a little fun at my own carefully cultivated antisocial existence. I say things like, "People annoy me; I don't get them; hermits have it made; if it weren't for the people, this would be a great town; if there really is an eternal afterlife, I'll shoot myself..." That sort of thing. I convince myself that there are only two or three human beings in the world I can stand to be around for more than ten minutes, and even that small moment of time too often culminates in a skull-crushing migraine.

I don't know, then, why it should surprise me when I look around and realize that my world is splitting at the seams with people I love and who, inexplicably, love me back.

The best of them make me laugh, and ten minutes pass in a flash. And, unlike other writers who hate it when people come up and say, "What you should really write about is ..." I actually like it. So thank you to all my friends, family members, and fellow weirdos who in one way or another contributed to this book. Thank you for reminding me or telling me the one about the exploding gum-chewer, the one about the dead amigo at the check-cashing place, the one about the genius in the catapult, the one about the decapitated head on the hood of the Oldsmobile, and so many others. Most especially, thank you Holly, thank you Christopher, and thank you Alyssa.

Introduction

I suppose there comes a time in every life when we each begin to take seriously the notion that, no matter how many carrots we've eaten or thousands of miles we've jogged, we might actually die of something anyway. For some of us, it happens right around the time that AARP starts sending us mail, and our first reaction is, "Myrtle, get me my gun." For others, death as a personal experience is such an unimaginable concept that we banish it from all consciousness the moment it threatens to surface; we refuse to let it register.

The rest of us—a small minority perhaps, but we know who we are—obsess about death all our lives.

Some years ago, I took stock of all the ways in which the various dead members of my family had met their respective ends. It didn't take long to discover a pattern.

One of my grandfathers died of a massive coronary thrombosis, followed by a succession of cerebral hemorrhages. In other words, he imploded.

One of my grandmothers also died of a heart attack. I've often wondered whether she might have survived that unfortunate episode had she not been so utterly terrified of death. It's easy to imagine that what killed her was not the heart attack itself, but the fear that a heart attack would kill her. Ironically, it did.

In recent years, many members of my family have learned to eat their vegetables, work out, get regular checkups, and live past the age of forty-two. As a result, very few of us implode anymore. We now take much healthier bodies into maturity and beyond, where our brains slowly turn into vegetable dip.

As with so many families these days, Alzheimer's seems to have found a comfortable perch on one branch or another of my family tree. It's entirely possible that it's always been there, grinning slyly like a fiend, biding its time. We just didn't notice it before because, in previous generations, very few of us lived long enough to achieve dementia.

I ponder such causes of death quite often. I examine them in the context of my own life and possible mode of demise. I weigh them carefully, one in each hand, like a scale: Implosion, vegetable dip. Implosion, vegetable dip. Which will claim me first? Which would I prefer?

Although neither of these is particularly appealing, I'm not especially frightened by the prospect that either one could be hovering around the edges of my near or distant future, waiting to pounce. Frankly, I'm much more frightened of kangaroo rats. (I saw a picture of one in a book when I was six. No bogeyman ever scared me more. I still think it's one of Nature's most pointlessly horrifying inventions.)

Nevertheless, there's an interesting conundrum here: There are lots of things I can do to avoid imploding, or at least put it off for a couple of years. If I don't implode, then I'll likely live long enough to watch my marbles roll away one at a time while I smile sweetly and drink Ensure out of a sippy cup.

Lucky me.

Even those of us who have spent many years in thoughtful contemplation of such odds and possibilities know that there's no telling which version of the Reaper will actually show up one day and say, "Hey, you. C'mere." Still, that doesn't stop us from wondering.

I suspect that's really what's behind this admittedly sick hobby of collecting stories about weird deaths. I suppose that, deep down, I want to believe I'm going to be just a *leeetle* bit luckier than those poor slobs who get killed by their own pet goats or are punctured to death with an automatic nail gun. But there's something more: Weird death stories offer a bit of proof that there are indeed an awful lot of unlucky stiffs in the world, and that any one of them could be me. Such proof has turned out to be strangely life-affirming. I find that profoundly comforting, even in all its twistedness. It makes me want to savor every meal and tender moment that much more, instead of wondering whether I should try to clog my own arteries on purpose or just wait for my brains to turn to mush.

Something tells me you know what I mean.

—Cynthia Ceilán
New York City

CHAPTER

1

THE BEST LAID PLANS

I want my mortician to lay me out with a gigantic smile on my face. My eyes should be closed, of course, but the grin must be EPIC. I'm not talking about some dinky little shy imitation of a *Mona Lisa* half-smile. I want a great big honking, crazy-assed-happy, face-splitting, toothy grin. I would love to know that, at my funeral, not a single person was able to keep a straight face. Even better would be to know that many of them peed their pants laughing.

Now that's a funeral!

I've always admired people who managed to go out in their own wild and wooly style, thumbing their noses at tradition, and snickering gleefully from beyond the grave. There is nothing I find as delightfully inspiring as the guy who goes into that dark night festooned in feather boas and rhinestone dancing shoes, or the person whose wonderful friends and relatives are all too happy to honor their dearly departed's last wishes, no matter how outlandish. Which reminds me: I'm going to need one hell of an executor.

Russell Parsons of West Virginia is taking no chances. He survived cancer and a stint in the Army. Death doesn't scare him. What scares him is other people making mistakes on his behalf when he can no longer speak for himself.

In 2007, Parsons prepaid and made arrangements for his own cremation through the Barlow Bonsall Funeral Home. Still not satisfied that this was enough, Parsons took himself to a tattoo parlor and had some flames inked into his right arm with these instructions: "Barlow Bonsall: Cook 1700–1800° for 2 to 3 hours."

When Wayne Carraway's father passed away in 1995, Wayne promised to scatter the ashes along the old man's favorite fishing spot, an area called the Fakahatchee Strand in the Florida Everglades. Wayne decided to give himself a little time to grieve properly.

Twelve years later, he finally got around to moving the cedar box containing the plastic bag full of dear old Dad's cremains from a cupboard in the house to the backseat of his Ford Bronco.

Sometime between Sunday night and the Monday morning of May 21, 2007, someone broke into the locked Bronco. Wayne found the cedar box overturned on the lawn, and the plastic baggie ripped open. What was left of Dad was scattered all over the lawn.

Wayne and his wife gathered as much of the cremains as they could. Wayne said he would scatter the ashes along the Fakahatchee Strand. Someday.

In 2004, a forty-six-year-old man from Washington state told his family that when he died, he would like to have his ashes scattered over a cemetery in Forrest Grove, Oregon, where many of their deceased relatives were buried. In this manner, it would be like being able to spend eternity with everybody he loved.

When he passed away of natural causes not long after this conversation, his surviving relatives did their best to honor his wishes. They had him cremated and soon afterward rented a small plane. As they circled the Forrest Grove cemetery, the bag of ashes slipped out of their hands and plummeted to the earth—and blasted a hole through the roof of Barbara Vreeland's house.

Mrs. Vreeland initially thought it was a terrorist attack and ran out of the house, but neighbors reassured her that they had seen something fall from the small plane flying overhead. When she later learned the whole story, she said, "I feel for those people, but I think some of their relative is still in our attic."

Bredo Morstoel lived his whole happy life in Norway. He was a great lover of outdoor winter activities, and worked as a director of parks and recreation for more than thirty years. But the real fun began when Bredo died of a heart attack in 1989.

Bredo's family packed him up in dry ice and shipped him to a cryonics facility in California where, dipped in liquid nitrogen, he was carefully kept for the next four years. In the meantime, his daughter Aud Morstoel and his grandson Trygve Bauge became huge advocates of cryonics. They dreamed of someday opening their own facility in their adopted hometown of Nederland, Colorado. In 1993, they prepared a shed in Trygve's backyard for their first customer: Grandpa Bredo.

A couple of years later, Trygve was deported back to Norway when authorities discovered that his visa had expired. Soon afterward, Aud was facing eviction for living in a house with no plumbing or electricity. A local reporter got wind of the story and helped convince the city council to make a special exception to the law prohibiting people from keeping corpses in their homes.

And so was born Frozen Dead Guy Day.

Every year in March, the town of Nederland welcomes weirdos from all over the world who come to celebrate the end of winter with parades, festivals, psychic readings, and polar bear plunges into icy waters, and to drink to the undying legacy of frozen Grandpa Bredo.

Bo Shaffer was the man Trygve hired as the caretaker, or Ice Man. Once a month, he and a team of volunteers go up to the old shed and dump 1,600 pounds of dry ice on Grandpa Bredo's sarcophagus. Bredo Morstoel may very well be the world's most beloved corpse.

Ted Cassidy was the actor best remembered for his role as "Lurch" in the original *Addams Family* television series from the 1960s. Lesser known is the fact that he also played "Thing"—or, more accurately, his *hand* played "Thing."

Poor "Lurch" died in 1979 at the age of forty-six, shortly after undergoing heart surgery in California. His girlfriend had his body cremated and then buried the urn in the front yard of the home they shared in Woodland Hills, California. Sometime later, she moved away and apparently forgot to take the ashes with her.

Rumors circulated for a while that some gardeners found the urn and kept it. Cassidy's final resting place remains a mystery.

When news got out in late March 1999 that the internationally acclaimed pianist Friedrich Gulda had dropped dead of a heart attack at the Zurich airport, world-class musicians and other luminaries from around the globe lined up to pay tribute to the genius and eccentric who had once played a duet on television with his girlfriend in the nude. But rumors of his demise were greatly exaggerated, mostly by Gulda himself. It is widely believed that he faxed the "news" of his own death to the Austria

Presse Agentur news agency from the Zurich airport because he wanted to read his own obituary.

Two weeks after the news item was published and immediately retracted by the APA, he played a Mozart concert in Salzburg titled "Resurrection Party." The concert was sold out.

❧

About one hundred people attended the funeral of fifty-two-year-old Holton Fleck, formerly of Los Angeles. Holton was a nudist, and so was his wife, Cindy Fleck, who made all of the arrangements in accordance with her late husband's wishes.

The 1997 affair was believed to be the world's first funeral in which the deceased, all of the mourners, and the officiating minister honored the memory of their dearly departed wearing nothing but their somber expressions.

❧

Nicky Swiggs wanted to do something truly memorable to honor his father's memory. George Swiggs, a sixty-eight-year-old farmer, died on October 26, 2008, leaving behind eight adoring children and a wife he had cared for and loved for thirty-six years. So Nicky and his fiancée, Sharon, came up with a really big idea: a hayride.

It was about a half-hour trip from the Swiggses' farm to the church, so they put George's coffin on top of a trailer loaded with hay bales and hitched the trailer to a tractor. Then as many of the family intrepid enough to climb onto the trailer rode along with the coffin. The whole way to the church, George's favorite song, "The Wurzel's Combine Harvester," played on the boom box.

His mother-in-law, eighty-five-year-old Peggy Matthews, said, "It is very unusual," and fretted about what other people would think. But in the end, even she came around and agreed it was more fun than a regular funeral.

❧

Gram Parsons was a pioneer of country rock in the 1960s and 1970s. He played with the Byrds, the Flying Burrito Brothers, and a number of other bands. Gram was also a serious dope addict who happened to love Joshua Tree National Park in California. It was his favorite place to get high, commune with nature, and search for UFOs. He loved the place so much he wanted to be laid to rest there someday, even though it is illegal to bury a corpse in a national park. Gram made his wishes known to his closest friends anyway.

Gram died of a drug overdose in 1973. His road manager, Phil Kaufman, and another friend had promised Gram that they would scatter his ashes at Joshua Tree National Park. So they borrowed a hearse and stole Gram's coffin from the Los Angeles International Airport. They took the casket into the park and set it on fire.

Cremating a body by setting the coffin ablaze turned out to be a lot more difficult than it looked. Phil and his cohort were arrested a few days later. They were ordered to pay a $700 fine for burning the coffin but were not charged with body snatching. Lucky for them, stealing a body was not a crime in California.

In 1916, the Fifth Avenue Coach Company created a funeral bus to solve the pesky traffic-clogging problem of long funeral processions. The bus could accommodate up to two dozen bereaved friends and relatives plus, of course, the dead guy in the coffin.

On its final trip in San Francisco, while transporting a funeral party up a hill, the bus tipped backward. The coffin, corpse, and all of the mourners tumbled all over one another. From that point forward, long, traffic-clogging funeral processions seemed the better option.

The funeral bus was parked and sold to a California cowboy, who moved into it and made it his permanent home.

❧

It is believed that England's first-ever funeral held in a theater was the one organized for Graham Frood, who helped to found the Unity Theatre in Liverpool in the 1930s. The curtain came down for the last time for Frood on September 29, 2003.

❧

Allan Young, a thirty-nine-year-old man from Castlemilk, Scotland, was having a very bad year. He was serving six months at HM Prison Barlinnie in Glasgow for driving with a suspended license. Then his girlfriend died when she got hit by a truck. And not long after that, his dear sainted mother passed away.

Allan was granted permission to attend his mother's funeral, but there was a miscommunication somewhere along the line. The three guards assigned to escort the docile prisoner showed up several hours late, causing Allan to miss the entire event.

His family begged the staff at the crematorium to wait a bit longer before putting Mrs. Young into the furnace. The staff obliged. Allan and his guards finally did show up, and he was allowed to stand as one of his mother's pallbearers. The act was as awkward as it was sad because Allan was still chained to one of the guards.

Allan's family filed formal charges with the state.

❧

When Milton Martin died in the summer of 2000, his buddies loaded his coffin onto the flatbed of a tow truck and began the procession from the Norris Funeral Home to the North Cemetery in St. Charles, Illinois. Seventeen other tow trucks joined the solemn procession. They had come from all corners of Illinois to honor one of their own. "That's what happens when someone owns a towing company," said Milton's son, Lonnie Marshall. "Lots of other companies wanted to send a truck," he added, "but Monday is a busy day for the towing industry."

❧

Chris O'Neil of Colorado was feeling dejected over her recent divorce, the loss of her job, and the mysterious death of her cat, so she called her sister Karen Katz in California. In that August 12, 1999, conversation, Chris also told her sister that she had had a very disturbing dream. In this dream, their mother had tried to strangle her, so Chris had smothered her with a pillow to save herself.

Karen became suspicious when, after several days, she was unable to contact her mother by phone. She asked the Arapahoe County sheriff to stop by the house Chris shared with their mother.

No one was home when officers arrived. A deputy peeked through a basement window and saw an oblong cardboard box surrounded by teddy bears, flickering candles, and wilting roses. Officers secured a search warrant and broke into the house. When they opened the cardboard box, they found sixty-five-year-old Martha Burns packed in seven hundred pounds of salt. The salt had sucked most of the moisture from the corpse, leaving it in a state of partial mummification. She had been dead for about a week.

More than twenty years before, Roger Caldwell, who was Chris's father and Martha's ex-husband, had killed his own mother-in-law, eighty-three-year-old heiress Elisabeth Congdon, by smothering her with a satin pillow. He also bludgeoned a nurse to death with a brass candlestick when she tried to save Ms. Congdon.

Chris O'Neil was found about a week after the discovery of her mother's salted corpse. Chris had parked her car in the garage of an upscale town house that was under construction in an area just south of Denver. She put one end of a rubber hose into the car's exhaust pipe and the other end inside the car. She sealed the gaps in the windows with duct tape and sucked on carbon monoxide until she was dead.

A man named Peter Marsh from Dublin, Ireland, might have lived and died in total obscurity if not for the terrible fuss he made about his premonitions about his own death. He was attacked by a crazed horse one day in 1740, and the horse dropped dead a few days later. Marsh became convinced that he, too, would die of whatever mental illness had overtaken the horse.

Marsh did, in fact, die not long afterward. The obituary that appeared in a publication called *Gentleman's Magazine* said that Marsh died because he had driven himself crazy. It is far more likely that he died because he had been hit by an out-of-control horse.

In 1988, Sheryl Jesswein booked the Chapel of Chimes at the Wisconsin Memorial Park cemetery as her wedding venue. She wanted to be near her deceased father on the most beautiful day of her life. When she told her fiancé, he freaked out and dumped her.

Two years later, she met Kurt, who thought the idea was "pretty neat." Most of his relatives were (or would soon be) buried there, so it seemed the perfect spot. On their wedding day, Sheryl placed her hand on the mausoleum niche where her father's cremains sat. "It was like he was giving me away," she said.

Sheryl and Kurt have already purchased their own cremation niches at the same mausoleum. They're looking forward to spending eternity in the same spot where they were wed.

There is a funeral service in Northumberland, England, called Blackhawk Hearse. Its sole purpose is to provide cortege services for dead motorcyclists.

Blackhawk uses a specially built and elaborately adorned, black and gold, ten-foot-long hearse, similar in appearance to a Wild West stagecoach. The hearse is hitched to a tricked-out 1450cc Harley-Davidson tricycle. A funeral procession led by this one-of-a-kind hearse followed by a procession of Harleys is a sight to behold.

Chef Brian Price tried to make the best of a bad situation. His job was to cook the last meals for death row inmates at the Huntsville jail in Texas. To his chagrin, most prisoners' requests were rarely more imaginative than an ordinary hamburger. But Chef Price didn't let that stop his own creativity in the kitchen. He experimented with a variety of interesting sauces to serve with "the usual," figuring that if any convict objected, he'd probably be dead before he could lodge a formal complaint.

Chef Price's creations, however, became quite popular. In 2005, he collected his recipes and published a rather unique cookbook. He considered a number of possible titles, including *Dead Man Forking* and *The Condemned Man's Cookbook*, but finally settled on *Meals to Die For*. The book includes stories about some of the more than two hundred inmates whose last meals he cooked and copies of a few of the prisoners' handwritten requests. The names of some of the recipes are just as delightful. Most notably, Rice Rigormortis.

The widowed Queen Victoria of England famously mourned the death of her beloved Prince Albert for more than forty years. She had fallen in love with him at first sight, despite the fact that her first sighting of him was in a photograph and that he was her cousin. Even more incomprehensible to the less charitable among us was that he was a "beautiful" man, and she herself was short, dumpy, and rather homely.

In her widowhood, Victoria sought refuge in two things: The first was food, which made her morbidly obese. The second was a scandalously close relationship with her devoted manservant, the kilted, red-whiskered Scottish Highlander John Brown. It was widely rumored that Victoria and John Brown were secret lovers, though many dispute this claim, citing a lack of hard evidence.

Victoria's last wishes did little to dispel the rumors of her relationship with John Brown or to cause anyone to question her devotion to the memory of her beautiful consort, Albert. With her in the coffin are her late husband's dressing gown, a plaster cast of his hand, and a picture of John Brown, among other keepsakes.

She lies entombed beside Prince Albert in an extravagantly ornate mausoleum at Frogmore Gardens. The sarcophagus that rests atop the double tomb, carved from a single piece of flawless gray Aberdeen granite, is a larger-than-life effigy of Albert and Victoria as they looked at the time of Albert's death. They are depicted lying side by side, dressed in all their splendiferous regal finery.

Barbra Streisand's dog, the late Sammy the poodle, received the sort of tribute for which some of her most devoted fans would gladly have given ten years of their own lives. During a rare television appearance on *The Oprah Winfrey Show* in October 2003, Barbra sang "Smile" through sloppy tears and the massive lump in her throat while pictures of Sammy flashed on the giant screen behind her. The song, originally written by Charlie Chaplin, was later adopted by the Humane Society as the official anthem for their Kindred Spirit program for people who have experienced the loss of a beloved pet.

Margaret and Donald Beaton of Inverness, Scotland, loved traveling abroad, and did so throughout the many years of their marriage. When Donald passed away at the age of seventy-one in 2003, Margaret spent the last year of her life missing her beloved companion and regretting that they had never made it to some of the countries that had long been on their wish list.

Two years later, to honor his mother's adventurous spirit, Glen Beaton posted a listing on eBay. He offered small quantities of Margaret's ashes for free, asking only that she be scattered respectfully in all of the far-flung countries she would have liked to visit. His goal was to scatter his mother's earthly remains throughout as much of the planet as possible.

eBay withdrew the listing shortly after it first appeared, but not before Margaret's ashes made it into the hands of bidders in the United States, Canada, and Australia.

❧

Contrary to popular belief, Wolfgang Amadeus Mozart was not buried in a pauper's grave. It was indeed a communal grave in which multiple bodies were dumped, as was the custom of the time and standard practice for a number of reasons: First, space was scarce in Vienna in the eighteenth century. Second, the Emperor Joseph II had decreed that dead bodies and all of their germs should be dumped at least three and a half miles from Vienna proper. Lastly, only the names of dead aristocrats were allowed to be written on the cemetery wall. Everyone else just needed to be put underground as soon as possible.

Nevertheless, a gravedigger named Joseph Rothmayer, who had known Mozart, recognized the body of the young genius, who was only thirty-five when he died in 1791. Rothmayer could not live with the knowledge that such a man would not be memorialized in some significant way. So Rothmayer tied a piece of wire around Mozart's neck to mark it, knowing that another common practice of the time was to clear out old graves every ten years or so to make room for more corpses.

In 1801, when that particular grave was being cleared, Rothmayer claimed that he had located and salvaged Mozart's skull. He kept it in his home and preserved it as best he could, despite the fact that the lower jaw was missing.

Sometime later, presumably after Rothmayer's death, a certain Herr Radschopf came into possession of the skull, which he gave to a man named Jacob Hyrtl in 1842. When Jacob died, his brother Joseph Hyrtl inherited the skull.

Hyrtl's widow kept it until her own death in 1901. It was then bequeathed to the Mozarteum in Salzburg. However, the curators never believed it was really Mozart's skull, so they stuck it in a drawer and paid no more attention to it. Museum employees often reported hearing faint sounds of music coming from the drawer.

In 2004, researchers got permission to perform DNA tests to see if they could conclude one way or the other if the skull did indeed belong to the great composer. They exhumed the remains of two corpses that had been interred in a family mausoleum in Salzburg's Sebastian Cemetery, allegedly those of Mozart's grandmother Euphrosina Pertl and a teenage niece named Jeanette.

All the fuss turned out to be for naught. The DNA tests were inconclusive. It could not be proven that the lack of a clear match was because the skull was not Mozart's after all, or because the people in the family vault were not who they said they were. Identity theft among the dead was also a rather common occurrence in those days. People who could not bear the thought of being buried in communal graves and forgotten forever often arranged to have their survivors pass themselves off as members of a more prominent family in order to ensure interment in fancier surroundings. It is just as likely that the two female skeletal remains belonged to more distant members of Mozart's family, or people who were not biologically related to Mozart in any way.

Either way, the current curators of the Mozarteum are considerably less flippant than their predecessors. The skull is locked in a safe in a secure place at the museum ... just in case.

~

When the German countess Carlotta Liebenstein died in 1992, she left $60 million to her dog, Gunther III, and named an obscure European pop band called The Burgundians as guardians of her beloved German shepherd and his inheritance. The band turned out to be better at making wise investments than they were at making music; they only released one record and sold not a single copy. However, Gunther III lived out the rest of his life in the manner to which he had always been accustomed—in the warm lap of unimaginable luxury.

When Gunther III died, his son, Gunther IV, inherited the fortune, now worth more than $180 million.

🐌

Hunter S. Thompson, the father of gonzo journalism (blending fact and fantasy in telling a true story with the writer at the center of the action), shot and killed himself at the age of sixty-seven on February 20, 2005. His suicide note had a title: *Football Season Is Over*. It was short, sad, and full of a terrible, palpable weariness.

Thompson's funeral plans, on the other hand, were a work of joyful exuberance.

Thompson had been planning his own send-off for more than thirty years. Six months to the day after his death, three hundred of his closest friends and family gathered at his farm outside of Aspen, Colorado, to celebrate the man who had lived his entire life flying in the face of all that was ordinary.

A 153-foot artillery cannon was erected according to the blueprints Thompson had asked his friend, the talented illustrator

Ralph Steadman, to create. The Gonzo Fist Memorial, described by *Rolling Stone* magazine as "a pyrotechnics-rigged mausoleum," was loaded with ten mortar shells into which Thompson's ashes had been packed along with the gunpowder. After the eulogies were delivered, the cannon was fired up.

Thompson was blasted into the air alongside an impressive array of fireworks that lit up the Colorado night against a full moon. "Spirit in the Sky" blared from high-decibel speakers. The ashes rained down all over the farm, and on all those gathered to honor the memory of their friend.

It may be awhile before anyone tops this one.

2

DYING FOR A LIVING

Just about everyone I know has at one time or another uttered the words, "This job is killing me," or something to that effect. I've known people who love what they do and can't wait to hop out of bed and start a new workday (or so they say, the crazy bastards), but even they have days when things don't go as smoothly as they'd like.

Everybody's had at least one less-than-competent boss, a co-worker who knows exactly how to unravel your last good nerve, an important tool or piece of equipment that breaks down mere minutes before a career-ending deadline, or a client who makes you wish it were within the bounds of business etiquette to hit someone across the face with a flat-blade shovel.

On the bright side, sometimes the job *can* kill you. On your most horrible day on the job, at least you'll have that to look forward to.

Nicholas Atfield, a thirty-one-year-old dockworker from Devon, England, was unloading a massive catch from a sixty-foot boat called the *Emma Jane* when she returned to Salcombe Quay from her two-day crabbing expedition in December 2008. He somehow got caught in a cable and was dragged into the winch and crushed to death.

Chris Venmore, secretary of the South Devon and Channel Shellfishermen Association, said, "A lot of us have lost bits and pieces in the winches," and showed the reporter his chopped-off thumb.

In September 2008, wood slabs jammed a conveyor belt at the Cousineau Wood Products plant in North Anson, Maine. The jam caused the machinery to come to a complete halt. A fifty-three-year-old production manager named Monte Jackson climbed up a catwalk, carefully made his way across an I-beam, and reached over to loosen the boards. He was only a few feet above the concrete floor, but he lost his footing and landed on his head. He was killed instantly.

🦎

Buapha Kumthawa, a forty-one-year-old laborer originally from Thailand, was working at a construction site in Menglembu, Malaysia, in February 2003. He and three of his coworkers were fastening a number of iron rods to a cable to load them onto the iron bucket of a bulldozer. The bucket suddenly swung around and hit Buapha in the head. He was dead before he knew what hit him.

🦎

Michal Holowczak, a Polish immigrant working as a construction laborer in Passaic, New Jersey, in 1995, was helping to load large chunks of concrete into a dump truck. The small team of laborers was doing some work at a private residence and made a judgment call: The pieces of concrete were too large to throw over the side of the truck, but renting a backloader was too expensive and not worth the cost given the relatively small number of chunks they needed to haul away. So they propped open the dump truck's 450-pound tailgate with a two-by-four piece of wood.

Michal threw a large piece of concrete onto the back of the truck and accidentally knocked off the two-by-four. The tailgate came crashing down on top of his head. He was pronounced dead at the scene.

*

The tiny Cornish village of St. Ewe has a total population of forty. Well, more like thirty-nine.

On April 15, 2008, paramedics were called to the Polmassick Vineyard to help dig out sixty-six-year-old George Musgrave from under an avalanche of bottles. The beloved winemaker and his wife were standing at the back of a truck that was unloading bottles when a half-ton pallet got loose. It flew off the back of the truck and crushed Mr. Musgrave to death.

*

A Mexican meat-processing plant in Mexico City kept a couple of unusual pets. A lion and a tiger lived in a cage on the roof of the facility. The animals were well cared for and healthy, though many people would agree that this was probably not the best home for such exotic creatures.

Angel Aguilar, a fifty-six-year-old employee of the plant, was in charge of feeding the big cats. On June 4, 2007, he went up to the roof to give a few pieces of chicken to his charges.

The lion took a giant swipe at the man and dragged him screaming into the cage. The tiger immediately perked up and went over to help. The two of them were much more interested in Aguilar than in a few measly pieces of chicken.

Paramedics arrived quickly but were unable to get past the cats to rescue Aguilar, who was still alive but at the mercy of the animals. When there was nothing left of Aguilar but a bloody pile of rags, the lion and the tiger settled down a bit. This gave the animal protection workers an opportunity to sedate them. They tied the tiger's muzzle shut with a block of wood in its mouth, put both animals in a van, and transported them to a nearby zoo.

The tiger was dead on arrival; it had suffocated in its makeshift muzzle. The lion survived.

🐾

British actor Ford Kiernan thought he had killed his costar, a Clydesdale horse named Mack, by overfeeding him cheese sandwiches. Kiernan and the animal were at odds all day while shooting *Dear Green Place,* a popular BBC sitcom, in the fall of 2007. Kiernan, who spoke openly of his lifelong equinophobia, said that Mack was no ordinary Clydesdale, a breed famous for its strength and docility. "That particular horse spent the whole day taking bites out of me," he said. "My knuckles were in tatters." Shortly after the film shoot, the crew found the horse dead. Kiernan worried that Mack might have suffered from high cholesterol and that the cheese accelerated its demise. An autopsy later revealed that the horse died of cancer.

Neil Mojica and Eduardo Molina, two Filipino shipyard workers, were moving an overhead crane to another location on the wharf in March 2008. When they detached the chains from the framework, the crane immediately became unstable, toppled over, and fell to the ground, landing on its flat steel-platform side. Unfortunately, it landed in exactly the same spot where Neil and Eduardo were standing. The crane flattened them both.

John Quinton Moffatt was a ten-year member of the Green and Clean Team, a garbage collection unit in the town of Morpeth, England. The fifty-one-year-old man was working his usual residential route on an icy day in January 2006. When he stepped out of the truck in front of a house on Spelvilt Lane, the truck suddenly rolled forward, crushing him to death.

🐛

Alcwyn Jenkins, a seventy-two-year-old man from Wales, was a longtime cricket umpire and great lover of the sport. In July 2009, he was working at a game between Swansea and Llangennech, which drew an unusually large crowd of spectators. In the middle of the game, a batsman hit the ball to a boundary, and a fielder threw it back to the wicket. The ball came flying so fast that Jenkins never saw it. It hit him on the side of the head, killing him instantly.

🐛

A welder at an iron ore plant in Beijing was killed when the cell phone he was carrying in his pocket exploded. The 2007 incident launched an investigation into Motorola batteries, which officials believe caused the freak accident. Motorola adamantly denied that any of its products, even at high temperatures, were capable of exploding. A company spokesman suggested that the unfortunate welder was probably using a fake battery, or maybe even a knockoff Motorola phone, both of which are plentiful throughout China.

☙

Betty Stobbs was a tough and fearless sixty-seven-year-old sheep farmer from Stanhope, England. Ordinarily, sheep are not animals that inspire much fear or that are known for being particularly bright. However, as Betty learned a bit too late, when sheep are hungry, all bets are off.

Betty rode up to the meadow on her motorized bike one afternoon in 1999, with her faithful collie trotting alongside. When the sheep saw her coming, they charged in her direction. Betty tried to outmaneuver the approaching stampede, but they forced her over a hundred-foot drop and into a ravine.

The coroner surmised that Betty actually survived the fall but was crushed to death when the motorbike fell on top of her.

☙

On December 22, 1916, lighthouse keeper Frederick Jordan drowned when his boat capsized just outside the Penfield Lighthouse off the coast of Fairfield Beach in Connecticut. Rudolph Iten, who was Jordan's assistant, took over the job. Iten diligently documented the death of his former boss in the official log and went about the business of keeping ships safe from the rocky shores.

Two weeks later, Iten reported seeing Jordan's ghost gliding down the spiral staircase. When he went to his log to document the occurrence, he found the book open to the entry describing Jordan's death.

According to several reputable and trusted lighthouse keepers who took over the job, keeper Jordan made many appearances in the decades following his death. A number of boaters who got caught in particularly nasty weather in the vicinity of the lighthouse also made official reports of a "mysterious stranger" who suddenly appeared to render aid and then just as quickly vanished once the hapless seafarers were safely back on shore.

In 2007, the U.S. General Services Administration put the lighthouse up for sale—for $1, in as-is condition, and with the possible inclusion of a ghost.

🖎

Fernando Jimenez Gonzales was working at the Coastal Circuits Factory, a circuit board manufacturing facility in Redwood City, California. Part of the process involves dipping circuit boards into sulfuric acid to remove any excess copper. In September

2007, Fernando walked up to a waist-high vat of sulfuric acid without his protective facial gear. He was immediately overcome by the fumes, passed out, and fell into the vat. Technically, the cause of death was drowning. Without a face or internal organs, it was difficult to determine any other cause of death.

❧

Terri Castle insisted it was an accident when she ran over and killed Lana Hanson in West Virginia in 2005. She said she didn't see Lana step directly in front of her car. When that explanation failed to hold water, she said she was following Lana because the woman had tried to rob her. Prosecutors convinced a jury that Terri drove her automobile over Lana to get out of paying off a debt incurred over a drug deal.

❧

Selling old copper tubing can be a lucrative enterprise for salvage operators and some sticky-fingered entrepreneurs. In October 2007, a German thief thought he had hit the mother lode in the city of Duisburg. He had already accumulated quite a few yards of copper cable when he put his metal cutters to a live wire. The ten thousand volts of electricity incinerated him beyond recognition.

The only part of the thief that remained uncharred was the hand that had been blown off his wrist with the force of the shock. Police used the hand to conduct a fingerprint search. As luck would have it, the thirty-two-year-old had a long history of theft in that part of Germany.

~

Mary Marie Hagan of Killyleagh, Ireland, worked the evening shift at a carpet factory. She had twenty years of experience in the industry. At the end of the shift one night in January 2000, her coworker Samuel Patterson noticed she was sitting too close to the yarn-spinning machine she operated. He went to see if something was wrong and noticed that her hair and apron had become entangled in the machine. The yarn spinner had strangled her.

The machine itself was a simple piece of equipment that posed virtually no danger to the operator. The coworker who freed Mary Marie from the machine didn't even have to turn it off to disentangle her.

No one knew how long she had been sitting there, trapped by the machine, or why she didn't simply reach over to the nearby handbrake that would have shut the equipment down immediately and released her.

&

A Romanian priest, identified only as Father Daniel, and four nuns were arrested in June 2005 for the murder of Sister Maricica Irina Cornici. Members of the convent claimed that Sister Maricica was possessed by the devil, so they called Father Daniel in to perform an exorcism. He and the four other nuns tied the twenty-three-year-old woman to a cross, stuffed a rag in her mouth, and left her alone in a cold chamber in the convent as part of the ritual. Three days later, she was dead.

"I don't understand why journalists are making such a fuss about this," Father Daniel reportedly said. 'According to the priest, the exorcism was a success. Clearly, dead nuns are of limited use to a demon.

&

Martha Mansfield was a smoldering twenty-four-year-old beauty from the silent movie era. She was starring in a Civil War film called *The Warrens of Virginia* on location in November 1923. When she was done for the day, she walked past a cast mate who had carelessly thrown a lit match without realizing it had landed on her hoop skirt. Martha got into a waiting car unaware that she was smoldering—in the literal sense—and closed the door. Almost immediately, her entire costume combusted, turning the car's interior into a self-contained inferno. Martha died a few hours later as a result of her burns.

⁂

On December 21, 2007, sixty-six-year-old Ken Hendricks climbed up onto the roof of his garage to check on the progress of the work being done on his Rock, Wisconsin, home. He fell through the woodwork and onto the concrete floor below, landing on his head. He was pronounced dead on arrival at Rockford Memorial Hospital.

At the time of his death, Ken was worth $3.5 billion. He had made his fortune in the roofing business.

⁂

There are twelve very peculiar areas of the planet Earth in which a disproportionately high number of mysterious disappearances and unexplained phenomena have occurred. Of these areas, known as Vile Vortexes, the Bermuda Triangle is the most famous.

If you were to poke a stick straight through the middle of the Bermuda Triangle and through the core of the earth, the other end of the stick would emerge in an area of the Pacific Ocean called the Devil's Triangle. It was here that the plane piloted by Amelia Earhart in 1937 lost radio contact and then disappeared altogether.

In 1950, the Japanese government declared the Devil's Triangle a danger zone and limited sea and air traffic in this area. Two years later, however, they sent nine scientists and a crew of twenty-two to take the *Kaio Maru No. 5,* a research vessel, into these strange waters to see if they could find answers to some of the region's mysterious disappearances. All thirty-one people on board perished. No traces of them were ever found.

The U.S. Air Force also avoids sending pilots out over the waters of the Devil's Triangle whenever possible.

David Williams, the fifty-four-year-old head of the chemistry department at the Bishopston Comprehensive School in Swansea, England, resigned his post after a falling-out with his colleagues in December 2002. He then decided to file a civil lawsuit against the school, which he lost. He was ordered to pay all costs associated with the legal action.

He was never told exactly how much this would be, but the more he thought about it, the bigger the number became in his own head. At one point, he convinced himself that the debt exceeded the £250,000 (about $415,000) value of his house. When he tried to borrow £120,000 from the National Union of Teachers, a clerk reported that Williams was quite irrational in his inquiry. Williams was admitted to a psychiatric facility, where he tried—and failed—to drown himself in the bathtub.

Five days later, he was released from the facility. He went home, had a nice Sunday lunch, walked to a nearby nature spot, and stabbed himself repeatedly in the neck, face, and head with a filleting knife until he was dead.

The actual debt was later estimated to be about £40,000.

❧

Santiago Ortiz, a forty-two-year-old farmworker from La Paz, Bolivia, decided to take a little nap under a fragrant Palo Santo tree. He had had a bit too much to drink that day in July 2009. The sweet aroma of the beautiful trees attracted many living creatures, including hoards of relentlessly aggressive red army ants.

When rescue workers arrived, Ortiz was already dead. The ants, however, were still munching away.

❧

Lisa Jane Brown, a twenty-seven-year-old nurse from Wales, sometimes had trouble waking up in time to get to work early. In 1998, she finally decided to get an alarm clock. When it rang in the morning, she was literally scared to death.

It took her parents seven years to find conclusive evidence that Lisa had a rare heart condition called Long QT, a disorder that can cause the heart's electrical system to malfunction. A sudden shock or frightening noise can easily stop such a person's heart.

When the diagnosis was confirmed, Lisa's sister immediately went out and got a pacemaker installed.

❧

Noel Lumley was happy to retire after twenty-five years as a technician at Eircom, an Internet service provider in Ireland. A well-loved neighbor and devoted husband and father, he went out to his work shed on his first day of retirement in March 2008 to prepare for a little yard work. While tinkering with the lawnmower, something sparked and set the entire shed ablaze. Lumley was consumed in the fire.

It is impossible to know if only the tiniest shift in circumstances would have made a difference. His official retirement date had actually been scheduled for the following week.

CHAPTER 3

SEND IN THE CLOWNS

The great existential philosopher Jean-Paul Sartre once said, "Hell is other people." Boy, was he right.

We all know people who will not rest until you are as unbearably miserable as they are. Even worse are the ones who are hell-bent on making sure everyone around them is as cheery and perky as they are.

I don't do perky. Perky makes me homicidal.

The most hellish of all people, however, has to be the archenemy of reason: the prankster.

It takes a special kind of weirdo to pull off a masterful practical joke. That person has to have just the right combination of brains, compassion, humor, and impishness, tempered with some real common sense. If any one of these elements is missing, the results can be disastrous, as any of the following people would tell you … if they were still alive.

Thiago Andrade Guedes, Mayderson de Vargas Mendes, and Ronald Ribeiro Rodrigues, three Brazilian friends in their early twenties, were aficionados of a murder-mystery role-playing game in which any one of the characters could "die," depending on how the game played out. One spring day in 2005, the three young men decided to raise the stakes and make the outcome truly interesting. They agreed that the loser and his family would become real murder victims. This is the story Mayderson and Ronald told Guarapari police when they found Thiago and his parents drugged, bound to their beds, and decomposing. They had been dead at least a week and a half.

An elderly man named Dhaniram (his only name) from the northern state of Uttar Pradesh in India had grown weary of his seventy-year-old wife's endless nagging. One Sunday afternoon in 2007, he tricked his grandson into helping him get a bit of revenge. He told the boy to scare his grandma with a toy gun but handed him a loaded pistol instead. Grandma died. Grandpa went to jail.

Mischief Night (aka Halloween) can get a little messy in certain neighborhoods. The New York City Metropolitan Transit Authority adds extra staff just to hose off the egg and other less palatable debris that is hurled at passing buses. Despite the city's valiant efforts to keep the windshields clean enough for the drivers to complete their routes, there's always at least one reveler who thinks he can get away with leaving his mark in some more permanent way.

On Halloween night 2009, twenty-two-year-old Bronx resident Luis Rivera hurled a large piece of wood at a passing bus. Unfortunately, Luis was no physicist, and so was rather unfamiliar with all that mumbo-jumbo about momentum and objects in motion. As he threw the piece of wood at very close range, his own body followed the forward trajectory, which caused him to collide with the wheels of the moving bus.

The driver reported that he felt some kind of bump on the left side of the bus. He stopped and got out to take a look. The

Unlucky Stiffs

bump, of course, turned out to be most of Luis Rivera. The rest of Luis was splattered all over the asphalt.

～

Jane Thomas worked as a care assistant at a retirement home in Birmingham, England. She was a warm and caring person, and known to be a bit of a jokester. At the end of her shift one cold night in December 1998, she offered her friend and coworker Marie Heath a ride home. The car was covered in frost, and the women began scraping ice off the windows and windshield. Marie then heard a bloodcurdling scream and immediately thought Jane was up to her old tricks. The car had moved and Jane was no longer standing on the other side of it. When Marie went around to the other side, Jane was gone.

Jane had reached into the car to turn on the engine and heater to speed up the process of deicing the windows. But when she had parked the car earlier that day, she had left it in reverse with the emergency brake off. When she turned the ignition, the car lurched, causing her to lose her balance. She fell and was crushed underneath the car. Jane was pronounced dead on the scene.

In the summer of 1874, a Rocky Mountain homesteader named Elijah Gibbs settled in the Colorado valley known as Brown's Creek with his wife and three children. One morning, he set out to make the acquaintance of nearby farmers. He stopped and tied his horses to a fence at a farm where the workers were threshing wheat. One of the workers was a practical joker named George Harrington. He talked the others into pulling the newcomer's horses into the threshing team while Elijah was otherwise occupied.

Elijah didn't think it was that funny. In fact, he flew into a rage and hurled obscenities at the men. When the dust had settled, nobody was laughing.

A few weeks later, Elijah and George got into another fight over a ditch. That night, George's outhouse went up in flames. When George ran outside to put out the fire, somebody shot him dead.

Elijah Gibbs was tried for murder but was acquitted in a Denver court.

The incident that started out as a sophomoric prank by a group of bored farmworkers continued to escalate over time. By the end of it was all, four more people would die: three men who tried to set fire to Elijah's house while he and his family were still inside, and the judge who refused to try him for the murder of those arsonists.

❧

Derek Jobes, a fifty-seven-year-old man from County Durham, England, was madly in love with his perky and endlessly fun-loving nineteen-year-old wife, Cassandra. They had been married only thirteen months, and she was just learning how to drive. In fact, she had had only two lessons. Still, on the evening of March 9, 2005, in the spirit of a good laugh, she thought she would give her husband a scare and drive off in his car.

Police and other drivers reported seeing a car matching the description of the one belonging to Mr. Jobes weaving in and out of traffic on the highway with the emergency blinkers flashing and the headlights turned off. The car almost ran over a motorist who had pulled over to change a tire. The car finally stopped when it crashed into a roundabout at Blind Lane, after it had rolled over a few times and flung Cassandra out one of the windows. She was pronounced dead at the scene.

Gareth MacFadyen worked for Merrill Lynch in Auckland, New Zealand. In December 2000, he made a tragic fashion choice: He wore a Hawaiian grass skirt to the office Christmas party.

The outfit was just too much for colleague Matthew Schofield to resist. While Gareth was in the men's room, Matthew reached under the door of the stall with his cigarette lighter.

Gareth's skirt went up in flames immediately, and so did Gareth. Another colleague, Angela Offwood, who just happened to be in the toilet, tried to beat out the flames.

Gareth died with his butt on fire, and Angela survived but was disfigured. Matthew pleaded guilty to manslaughter and unlawful injury. Rarely have office parties been more memorable.

Peter O'Flinn and Derek Clarke, both from Donaghmede, Ireland, were good buddies and coworkers employed at a Dublin shopfitters company. They were both well-liked and happy young men in their twenties who loved the occasional prank. One harmless pastime involved pulling the wipers up from the windshields of their respective cars.

On May 17, 2005, Peter did just that as he walked in front of Derek's parked car. Peter leaned over the hood from the front of the car and pulled the wipers up. Derek, who was inside, playfully let the car lurch forward. Peter fell backward onto the pavement, cracked his head open, and was crushed under the car.

The coroner ruled it an accident.

Terrence Quinn, a senior at Cornell University in 1993 and a member of the Sigma Alpha Mu fraternity, disappeared on January 15, 1993. He was found three days later when someone opened the flue at the Sigma Alpha Mu house and a pair of shoes and pants dropped onto the fireplace floor. The rest of Quinn was stuck farther up the chimney.

The young man was last seen drunk out of his mind outside a nearby bar. Although the timing coincided with the recruitment period known as rush, authorities were reluctant to characterize the event as a fraternity prank. Quinn might have taken it upon himself to surprise the members of the rival frat house but was too drunk to properly execute the stunt.

Lorraine Tedesco was affectionately known as the "Queen of the Rope" at the VIP Room of one of Miami's trendiest hot spots, Club Level. Originally from Scotland, Lorraine had come to America as an aspiring model. While working as a cocktail waitress, she met and married a handsome bartender named Philip, who harbored his own big dreams of becoming a famous model. By all accounts, they were a fun-loving couple, popular through their work in the fashion industry and the South Beach nightclub scene.

On December 9, 2001, they arrived home in the wee hours and decided to do a little fooling around. To add spice to their foreplay, Philip retrieved the gun he kept in his nightstand and pretended to be a marauder. In his excitement—and to his horror—he accidentally squeezed the trigger and put a bullet straight through Lorraine's heart.

Philip was charged with culpable negligence. The death was ruled an accident.

In 2000, a group of bored prison guards at the Feltham detention center in Middlesex, England, decided it would be fun to watch the inmates play gladiator games. To make things really interesting, they purposely put "natural enemies" together as cellmates—a black one with a white one, a big one with a small one, and so forth—and bet each other on how long it would be before a fight broke out.

Zahid Mubarek, who was just hours away from being released from the prison after serving a six-week sentence for petty crimes, was beaten to death with a table leg by Robert Stewart, an avowed racist. Stewart was diagnosed as a psychopath and is serving a life sentence for the murder. All of the officers accused of orchestrating the gladiator games are still working as prison guards.

∽

Emmett Cooke, Terry Kurosky, and Robert Keefer were all grown men in their forties from Fayette County, Pennsylvania. The three amigos carpooled to the construction site where they worked.

On the ride into work one morning in 2008, Robert was driving, Emmett was in the passenger seat, and Terry rode in the back of the car. They were traveling at a speed of about fifty miles per hour when Terry reached up from the backseat and pulled Emmett's hair, just for fun. So Emmett pulled the emergency brake, just for fun. Robert lost control of the vehicle, which went rolling down an embankment and came to a stop on its roof. When they looked back, Terry was gone, and so was the back window. The hair-puller had flown out of the car.

Terry died where he landed. Emmett went to jail.

Tom Gouvion didn't go to his buddy Elgin Rich's birthday party, because he had to work that night. Also, the party was at a bar, and he was still under the legal drinking age. So he waited until a smaller group gathered at Elgin's house in the wee hours of the morning of August 16, 1996, and had a couple of cans of malt liquor there.

They got hungry at about 3:30 in the morning and decided to go to a nearby restaurant for a snack. Tom was the least intoxicated of the bunch. In fact, his blood alcohol level was below the legal limit. So one of the friends, Bob Kraus, handed Tom the keys to his brand-new 1996 Chevy Cavalier and hopped into the backseat with Pamela Kanski. Elgin rode shotgun.

They were driving down North Sixtieth Street in Milwaukee at a pretty good clip, about fifty miles per hour, when Elgin got it into his head that it would be really funny to give Tom a "wet willie" (a spit-moistened finger in the ear). Elgin did it several times, causing Tom to swerve and drive erratically. The last wet willie is what did them in. Tom hit a tree dead-on. Elgin and Bob never made it out of the car. Pamela told the police, "The first thing through my head was, 'Bob's going to be real mad.'"

Tom was sentenced to four years in prison. The judge also ordered that he follow up the jail term with five years of probation, during which time Tom was to visit the graves of his dead friends and write letters to Elgin and Bob's bereaved parents after each visit.

A playground game of "slapsies" among a group of teens in a small town near Halifax, England, got a little out of hand in April 2008. Young Kyle Thompson was smacked in the face several times by his friends but got in a few good licks of his own before he was knocked to the ground and hit his head. As he lay there gasping, a girl came by and "playfully" kicked him in the stomach. So his friends picked him up and dropped him back on the ground, where the boy hit his head a second time. Police did not think the death was suspicious.

❧

Robert Hurt and Brandon Gish, two Bradley University students, were walking down a Peoria, Illinois, street in March 2008, behaving more like fifth graders than like men of higher learning. They kept trying to push each other into oncoming traffic. Brandon won. Robert died of massive head injuries.

❧

Jean Charles de Menezes, a twenty-seven-year-old Brazilian electrician living in the UK, was playing a game of chase with his friends as they made their way to work through the streets of Brixton in South London one morning in July 2005. Plainclothes police officers investigating the area for clues to recent bombings ordered Menezes to stop. Menezes thought the cops were a couple of new guys who had joined the game. The cops thought Menezes looked a bit too much like a Middle Easterner. They approached Menezes as he was about to board the train at the Stockwell Underground station and shot him five times at point-blank range. Scotland Yard relieved the shooting officer of his gun duties. The mayor blamed the whole thing on the terrorists.

On a hot August day in 2009 in Southern California, Jorge Valdez and a friend decided to cool off in the small swimming pool next to Jorge's girlfriend's trailer home. The two men soon began showing off and horsing around by wrestling underwater. After a little while, Jorge's girlfriend noticed that they had been down there an awfully long time and went into the house to get the other man's girlfriend. The women fished their men out with pool nets. Both men were half-dead from nearly drowning. That night at the hospital, Jorge died the rest of the way.

Hannah the Cow was killed in a tragic case of mistaken identity. The Michigan man who shot her in November 2007 told Undersheriff Rory Heckman that he thought Hannah was a coyote. That's his story and he's sticking to it.

Heckman reported that the perp had also tried to drag the 1,400-pound pregnant cow home with him. Authorities were considering bringing charges against the shooter because, whatever the circumstances, it is illegal to shoot coyotes during deer-hunting season.

CHAPTER

4

SHOULDA STAYED HOME AND ORDERED CHINESE

Do you ever get one of those funny feelings just as you're leaving the house, a little voice that says, "Why don't we just call in sick today?" Sometimes that little voice is wiser than we want to believe it is.

There aren't very many things that truly scare me in this life, but falling onto the subway tracks is definitely one of them. I'm one of those fraidy cats who loves public transportation but gladly hugs the wall, as far from the platform edge as possible, and waits patiently for the train to come to a full stop. I don't begin to move until the doors open.

This particular phobia was seriously exacerbated about ten years ago, on a day my little voice tried to talk me into staying home and I told it to shut up. I arrived at my subway station just as workers were pulling a soggy puddle of rags up from the rails. The puddle of rags had once been some poor slob who either lost his balance or got too close as the train arrived, and somehow got sucked into the space between two of the passing cars.

It would be nice to stay home all the time and have everything delivered. It would be nicer if that little voice really did have the power to predict when it was safe to venture outside or better to hide under the bed.

I don't know whether any of the people in the following stories had their own little voice, and if they did, why they chose to ignore it. But I would bet every one of them had one fleeting last thought that went something like, "Why in the world did I leave the house today?"

Richard E. Connor, a seventy-one-year-old man from Fort Wayne, Indiana, was feeding coins into a parking meter at about noon on February 2, 2007. A short distance away, a woman in a Kia van was rushing to beat a red light. She didn't quite make it. Her van hit the side of a Ford Ranger truck that was crossing the intersection. The truck spun out of control, took out a parking sign, a couple of meters, and Connor's Pontiac. The drivers of the van and the truck walked away without a scratch. Connor was crushed between the parking meter and his car. He was killed instantly.

Jerry Marcum and Richard Davis were traveling down Corridor G in Boone County, West Virginia, one night in 1993 when their car broke down. A young couple, Rebecca Cline and Jessie Norman, stopped to help. Jerry asked Rebecca to get a bottle of motor oil from the trunk of his car. When Rebecca said she didn't know what that looked like, Jerry called her a stupid bitch. So she pulled out a pink handgun and shot him in the head.

Yuchen Yeh of Woodcliff, New Jersey, drove to a nearby McDonald's on Route 17 for a late-night snack shortly before 1 a.m.

on January 27, 1994. He walked to the door and found that the sit-down area of the restaurant had already closed. However, the drive-through window was still open. So Yuchen started walking back to his car.

He probably never knew what hit him.

What hit him was a two-hundred-pound truck tire that had dislodged from a passing eighteen-wheeler, bounced, became airborne, flew over a three-foot highway divider, and struck him in the back of the head.

Police found the tire on an embankment about thirty yards away from Yuchen's body. Another tire, believed to be from the same tractor-trailer, was found farther south on the highway.

Four buddies in their twenties from Hobart, Australia, got drunk one night in May 2009 and decided to take in the view from the roof of St. Mary's Senior School for Girls. One of them fell through a skylight and landed on his head. He died a short time later at an area hospital. Authorities did not release his name but did say that the girls were offered counseling.

In February 2007, Ibrahim Yasin, a thirty-nine-year-old man from Malaysia, was traveling by motorcycle to Kampung Batu Peti with his twenty-two-year-old friend, Noraziman Johari, riding pillion. The bike swerved into the wrong lane and hit a car head-on. Both men died instantly in the crash. Ibrahim's head landed fifty feet away, in a grove of palm trees. It took rescue workers eight hours to find it.

Another biker named Md Zaidi Alias came upon the scene of the accident and stopped to help search for the head. He was killed by yet another motorcyclist on his way home.

The woman in the car in the first accident walked away unhurt.

Thirty-five-year-old music teacher Erica Brindley of Hervey Bay, Australia, took about fifty of her students on a class trip to Carnarvon Gorge in Queensland. They were all frolicking in a rock pool, having a wonderful time, when a eucalyptus tree fell directly on Brindley, killing her instantly.

Surangi Ratnaweera, a thirty-four-year-old medical doctor from Wrexham, England, was trying to work through some marital difficulties with her husband and was getting nowhere fast. Their frequent discussions often escalated into arguments, and the arguments threatened to break up the marriage. Tired of fighting one night in 2009, Surangi told her husband she was going to visit friends in London. On the way there, she stabbed herself in the groin, then crashed her car into a roadside barrier. Damage to the car was minimal. It was the uncontrollable bleeding from her femoral artery that killed her.

Joanne Mary Davidson and her family were vacationing with her family in Queen Charlotte Sound's Ngakuta Bay in New Zealand in January 2004 (the summer season in that part of the world). Joanne decided to "rough it" one night while her family opted to sleep in the great indoors. Joanne pitched her brand-new tent and fell asleep under stars. At some point in the night, a freakish gust of wind ripped her properly moored tent right out of the ground and sent her flying, a la *The Wizard of Oz*.

Rescue workers found the tent and a very dead Joanne the following morning, about twenty yards from the spot where she had pitched her tent.

Jim Fitzgerald was a retired policeman from the village of Sneem in County Kerry, Ireland. While driving home late one night, Jim spotted a neighbor emerging from a pub and offered him a ride home. Soon afterward, the car ran out of gas. The two men got out and began pushing the car. As they reached a bend, the car fell into a dyke, crushing Jim underneath. He died on the spot.

John Hutcherson and his buddy Frankie Brohm went out drinking one Saturday night in the summer of 2004. The two, now in their twenties, had been friends since high school. On the drive back to John's home in Marietta, Georgia, Frankie stuck his head out the passenger window of John's truck to puke. John, who was too drunk to drive in the first place, swerved and sideswiped a utility pole. He kept driving, though.

When John got home, he parked the truck and went to bed. The next morning, a neighbor noticed the bloody, headless body still inside the truck.

Frankie's head was found twelve miles away, not far from the utility pole. John was charged with vehicular homicide, leaving the scene of a fatal accident, and driving while intoxicated. He was sentenced to five years in prison.

Bernice Bouchie and her relatives had spent one fine spring day in 2008 getting sloshed in Bernice's home in Berens River in northern Ontario, Canada. Bernice's brother, sister-in-law, and niece decided to sleep it off on the front lawn. At about five o'clock in the afternoon, Bernice decided to go out for more supplies and ran over all three of them with her Pontiac Tempest. She killed her sister-in-law and was charged with vehicular homicide and driving while intoxicated. Bernice's brother and niece survived.

Christina Williams had amassed quite a reputation in her hometown of Dublin, Ireland, as a psychotic man-hater and violent drunk by the time she was twenty-five years old. It was poor Andy Foley's bad luck that he ran into her at a bar one lonely night in Dublin in May 2002.

Christina had been drinking since 7 in the morning when she approached fifty-one-year-old Andy that night. Pointing to a glass of Carlsberg beer, she said to him, "I'll bring you back for a fuck if you buy me that." Before she was actually ready to leave, she had downed nearly a dozen Carlsbergs, five pints of Guinness, and a double whiskey.

The two somehow stumbled to Andy's home together. Once there, he asked her to pony up on her offer of sex. Christina went into a psychotic rage. She stabbed Andy thirteen times with three different knives, gouging him in the eye, genitals, chest, and shoulders. She then finished him off with a kettle of scalding water.

At her murder trial she told the court, "I don't know why I did it. I just got carried away. I'm sorry. I did try to help him." She was sentenced to life in prison. She screamed obscenities at the judge and jury. The judge refused to hear her appeal.

🦎

Dorene Rodriguez, a driver for Spectrum for Living Adult Training Centers, picked up Rosario Dinaro on the morning of March

19, 2002, to take him from his hospital residence to a day-care center in Hackensack, New Jersey. While en route, the driver of a landscaping truck in front of Rodriguez's van made a sudden stop, barely missing his turn. Rodriguez slammed on the brakes and turned Dinaro into a human projectile. He flew out of his wheelchair and slammed headfirst into the van's engine compartment. The impact killed him.

꠸

Timothy and Thomas Willgruber, a fifty-six-year-old set of identical twins from Allentown, Pennsylvania, rarely went more than a day without seeing or speaking to each other. They were, by all accounts, best friends from birth. As they often did, the brothers decided to go out one evening in the fall of 2009. It's a pity neither of them thought to make the other the designated driver. Or the designated navigator. Or that they hadn't just stayed home and practiced their twin telepathy that night.

After a few drinks, Timothy was unable to parallel park the car, so Thomas got out to help navigate. Timothy lost control of the vehicle and plowed right into Thomas, pinning him to an SUV. Thomas did not survive the incident. In a manner of speaking, neither did Timothy. A few weeks later, he hanged himself.

Three elderly tourists traveling in Vietnam hired twenty-six-year-old Nguyen Van Hung as a tour guide in March 2004. They were traveling in Nguyen's jeep on a mountain road between Lao Cai and Sapa when they were stopped for a few minutes by a road construction crew. While they waited for the signal to move forward, a gigantic boulder fell from a higher elevation and landed squarely on the jeep, crushing three of the four people inside. In addition to the driver, Valerie Miles from Australia and Saper Arvay from the United States died instantly. The fourth tourist, also an American, miraculously escaped unharmed.

A police spokesman assured the press that there was, in fact, the occasional landslide, "but they rarely kill people, especially foreigners."

A fifty-nine-year-old woman whose identity was not released to the press went to visit an elderly couple living in the southwest region of Victoria, Australia, in January 2007. On her way up the rural drive, she stopped at the mailbox to retrieve any letters as a favor to the couple. However, instead of getting out of the car, she opened the door a bit and leaned out toward the mailbox. The car suddenly lurched forward and trapped her between the door and the frame. Half out of the car, she was unable to shift into reverse or otherwise free herself from the trap. Hours later, a passerby noticed something was amiss and called paramedics. She was long dead by the time help arrived.

Caspar, a twelve-year-old black-and-white cat well-known in his neighborhood and environs, liked waiting with commuters at the bus stop near his home in London, England. Caspar would often hop on the bus, make himself comfortable in one of the seats, and ride along for a while, or until he got bored. Bus drivers and passengers alike came to know him well over the years.

   While making his rounds one day in early 2010, Caspar was tragically killed by a hit-and-run driver. As news of his demise spread, condolences poured in from all over the world. The bus company announced it would pay tribute to Caspar's memory by including his picture on an advertisement on the side of the buses on the cat's favorite route.

T.J. Hickey, a young man from inner-city Sydney, Australia, had been in trouble with the law from time to time over such relatively small crimes as petty theft. On February 14, 2004, he was seen exiting a park on his bike, riding "like a bat out of hell" with a police paddy wagon in hot pursuit. As T.J. made a turn into a driveway, he became airborne, flew several feet, and impaled himself on a fence.

T.J.'s death sparked a series of violent riots in Sydney over alleged police brutality. Police denied they had been chasing T.J.

A runaway bull made its way onto a notoriously dangerous section of road on the A77 in Ayrshire, England, one night in August 2009. The bull was hit by an Audi traveling in the north-bound lane. It landed on the car and was carried a short distance before being thrown into the southbound lane, where it was hit by a Renault and finally by a Toyota.

When the emergency crew arrived, the drivers and passengers of the Audi and Renault were fine. The bull and the fifty-two-year-old guy in the Toyota, on the other hand, were dead where they landed. Neil Macgillivray, a communications manager for the Strathclyde Safety Partnership, told the press, "Striking any animal on a road, such as deer, can cause problems, but hitting a bull is very serious."

❧

Yesu Christy was very excited about his upcoming nuptials. He was especially happy to know that his beloved eighty-year-old grandfather, Thomas Valutham, had lived to see this day.

Shortly before the wedding, Yesu made the trip from his home in Klang, Malaysia, to his grandparents' house in the town of Siliau. Yesu brought them back to Klang for a large family gathering that was taking place that weekend in early August 2004. On Sunday, he drove them back to Siliau.

Yesu decided to park the car at a neighbor's house. He backed the car right into a wall. The trunk was open, blocking Yesu's view, so he didn't realize Thomas had been unloading his luggage from the back of the car. Yesu had crushed his own grandpa to death.

In accordance with Indian tradition, the wedding was post-poned for a year.

A sixty-one-year-old Croatian man identified as Tomislav K. boarded a late-night tram on June 3, 2007. He settled in for the ride home and promptly fell asleep. The following morning, at the end of the driver's shift, Tomislav was the only passenger still left on the tram. The driver tried to shake him awake, but he had been dead for hours. None of the passengers who had ridden the tram that night, including those who sat or stood next to the man, had noticed anything was wrong.

In 2007 in Oakland, California, the driver of a sport-utility vehicle struck a two-hundred-pound fire hydrant, dislodging it from its moorings and sending it hurtling through the air. The hydrant hit twenty-four-year-old Humberto Hernandez on the head as he crossed the street with his wife. It then hit a fence and traveled twenty more feet. Humberto died instantly. His wife and the driver of the SUV were fine.

By the mid-1830s, the indigenous population of the Channel Islands off the coast of Southern California had declined drastically since its first visit from explorers in the 1700s. Concerned for the welfare of the remaining people, priests from the Santa Barbara Mission made arrangements to find them and bring them to the mainland. Their hope was to save these people from starvation and total extinction.

In 1835, Captain Charles Hubbard and his crew boarded the *Peor Es Nada* ("Better Than Nothing") and headed for San Nicolas, the most remote of the Channel Islands. They loaded everyone they could find onto the schooner. One woman, however, could not find her young son, so she jumped overboard and swam back to the island. Captain Hubbard didn't much care one way or the other about one crazy woman, and set a course to sail back to the mainland where, as it made its way through the San Francisco Bay, the *Better Than Nothing* hit the rocks and sank. Almost everyone on board drowned.

Nearly twenty years later, a priest called Padre Gonzales managed to convince another ship's captain to return to San Nicolas to find the missing woman. He had been obsessing over her since first hearing that she had been left behind. A sea otter hunter named Captain George Nidiver and an Irishman named Charley Brown, known to everyone as "Colorado" (Red), accepted the challenge. Not long after their arrival, they spotted a strange old woman on San Nicolas, dressed in skins and feathers from the carcasses of dead cormorants. Once she lost her fear of the men, she shared her dinner of roasted onions with them, then happily joined them on their journey back to the mainland. As news of her rescue spread, she quickly became a celebrity. Unable to understand a single word she said, the priests named her Juana Maria.

Six weeks later, unaccustomed to her new diet and the trappings of modern civilization, Juana Maria dropped dead of dysentery.

⁂

In the summer of 2009, the *Sapphire Princess* cruise ship went on a whale-watching expedition off the coast of Alaska. When it docked in Vancouver, it had a seventy-ton whale lodged in the ship's bow, right at the waterline. The ship had dragged the whale a thousand miles or more.

No one on the ship noticed it had hit an obstacle, but as big as the whale was, it was no match for the 116,000-ton ocean liner. It would have been like a two-hundred-pound man bumping into a small wad of cotton balls.

Judging by the photographs, the ship collided with the whale's back at an almost perfect perpendicular angle, slicing about a third of the way through. Everyone hoped, for the whale's sake, that it died instantly.

Twenty-five-year-old Richard Stewart Jr. of Lake County, Indiana, was out partying with seven of his best friends one Saturday night in September 1995. They had rented a stretch limo for the evening.

At about 2 a.m., Richard opened the sunroof and climbed onto the top of the car. He was promptly thrown off the moving vehicle and landed headfirst on the pavement. Doctors at the Southlake Campus of Methodist Hospital identified Richard's massive skull fractures as the "possible cause of death." Considering what was left of Richard's head, it is unlikely there could have been any other cause.

Teryn J. Hutchins, originally from Wisconsin's Taycheedah Correctional Institution, where his mother was incarcerated for forgery at the time of his birth, was raised by relatives in Milwaukee.

In the summer of 1998, nineteen-year-old Teryn and his uncle Cornelius Earnest were playing a friendly game of craps with some other men. Teryn won a couple hundred dollars and quit the game while he was ahead, which didn't much please

Uncle Cornelius. Police say the two then engaged in a "friendly game of rock-throwing," after which Teryn went on his way.

The following evening, Teryn went to his grandmother's house and found Uncle Cornelius there. The two began arguing again over the outcome of the dice game. Teryn tried leaving in a friend's car, but Uncle Cornelius wouldn't let the matter drop. Teryn pulled out his gun to scare the man away, but the gun went off and killed Uncle Cornelius.

Teryn is back in the correctional system. He was sentenced to sixteen years.

Kimberly Bailey of Pomona, New York, went to the Jersey shore with her family in the summer of 1999 and rode the Wild Wonder roller coaster with her daughter Jessica at Gillian's Wonderland Pier. As it was making its thirty-foot ascent, the car suddenly lurched and began to move backward. It hit the car behind it with such force that Kimberly and Jessica were ejected from their harnesses. They were killed when they hit the ground.

The ride had been inaugurated on July 1 of that year. New Jersey Governor Christie Whitman herself pressed the button to send the roller coaster on its maiden run but refused to get into the machine when she was offered a free ride.

Sixty-three-year-old Agnetta Westlund of Stockholm, Sweden, went out for a quiet evening stroll in the forest in 2008. She was later found covered in blood, dead. Her husband, Ingemar, was the prime suspect and was jailed on suspicion of having murdered his wife. He spent ten days behind bars but was exonerated when lab tests revealed that the hair and saliva on Agnetta's clothing did not match Ingemar. The DNA belonged to a moose.

As a young boy, Skylar Deleon was an aspiring child actor who once appeared on the television program *Mighty Morphin' Power Rangers*. As an adult in real life, he was a bona fide homicidal maniac.

In November 2004, Tom and Jackie Hawks of Prescott, Arizona, decided to sell their fifty-five-foot yacht, the *Well Deserved*. Skylar showed up as an interested buyer. He arrived with a couple of buddies at the Southern California marina where the boat was anchored. Skylar asked to take the yacht out for a test run. Out on the open waters of the Pacific Ocean, the three poseurs overpowered the middle-aged couple, forced them to sign over the ownership papers, tied them to an anchor, and threw them overboard. The Hawkses' bodies were never found, but the artist formerly known as *Power Rangers* extra "Roger" was sentenced to death.

Just prior to his conviction, Skylar had tried to saw off his own penis with a razor blade. He was taken to the hospital, reconnected to his member, and returned to his cozy little jail cell.

In July 2008, Mr. and Mrs. Winfred Stafford, both in their late seventies, sat in their car in the parking lot of the Grace Assembly of God church in Oklahoma City, mesmerized by the sight of a crane installing a new steeple onto the roof of their beloved house of worship. Other people had gathered to watch, but the Staffords thought it would be safer if they stayed in the car. The crane suddenly toppled forward under the weight of its load. The steeple crashed directly onto the roof of the car, killing Mr. Stafford instantly. Mrs. Stafford, who was sitting in the backseat, escaped with minor injuries.

Charles and Linda Everson of Westland, Michigan, went to beautiful Lake Chelan in Washington state to celebrate their first wedding anniversary in 2007. On the drive back to their hotel one evening, a six-hundred-pound cow fell from a cliff and landed on their minivan. Charles and Linda were shaken but unharmed. The cow, on the other hand, was a gigantic mess. Animal control personnel had to euthanize it.

Boro Mandic, a twenty-nine-year-old man from Croatia, was counting his lucky stars after having narrowly survived a high-speed car crash in 2009. His automobile was totaled, but he walked away without a scratch. He was taken to the hospital and examined, then told he was good to go home.

No longer in possession of his wheels, he decided to walk home. The fog was thick on that December night, so he followed the train tracks to keep from wandering off course. He was run over and killed by an express train heading into Zagreb.

If forty-six-year-old Phillip Holman had had a home, he might have had a safe place to get drunk without endangering himself. Then again, a wanderer must wander, and his favorite place to enjoy a sip of cheap brandy was down by the train tracks in Huntsville, Alabama.

In September 2007, Phillip was hit by a train while on just such an excursion. Miraculously, he survived, but not intact. The train ripped one of his arms off and shattered one of his legs. Doctors were able to reattach his arm and straighten out his leg before sending him to the Downtown Rescue Mission to recover in relative comfort, or at least in a more hospitable environment than the railroad tracks.

Two years later, Phillip found himself once again drinking brandy by the tracks. This time, the Norfolk Southern train that hit him killed him instantly.

It's a big bad world out there, and staying home isn't always the cure.

In January 2009, a few hours after Robert Bryson and his wife, Lisa Kline, went to bed, Robert apparently went for a little stroll—in his sleep. Lisa woke up at about 1:30 in the morning to a terrible crashing sound. She found her husband in the yard outside their bedroom window, dead. He had fallen off the second-floor balcony and landed on a fence.

5

ALL GUTS, NO GLORY

"At least he died doing something he loved," is a familiar refrain among otherwise well-intentioned mourners at the funeral of someone who died in the middle of trying to do something fun.

Really? Somebody who gets harpooned by the swordfish he was trying to catch is happy he died that way? Or some poor slob who finds a few precious moments of enjoyment throwing darts at a board will gladly drop dead of a heart attack right there in the pub when his team finally wins one lousy little tournament?

Well, now that I think about it, maybe that's not such a terrible thing.

It is ironic, though, to think that the thing that gives us the most pleasure can also be what kills us. It certainly has to be better than dying in the middle of doing something you hate. Okay, so I take it back: It is better to die laughing or singing or dancing than to die while cleaning the office refrigerator.

Still, I don't envy the fates of the hapless heroes in any of these stories.

Donald and Rona MacKenzie of Bowmore, Scotland, went on their annual yachting trip with their good friend George Rhind in the summer of 1999. They set the anchor down one night in Arisaig Bay, off the western coast of Scotland. Donald decided to go ashore for supplies. He took his wife's life jacket and paddled off in the little inflatable dinghy.

When he returned, he brought the dinghy around to the side of his yacht. He lost his footing as he tried to exit the raft and fell into the water. The life jacket was doing a splendid job of keeping Donald from sinking, but unfortunately it was holding up the wrong end of him. Because the jacket was too small for him, Donald had not been able to fasten it properly. It slipped down his body, flipped him over, and kept him there. He drowned with his legs sticking out the water.

Randall Beasley and Rantwon Smith were playing dice in the hallway of a Syracuse, New York, apartment building in March 2008. Rantwon won all of Randall's money. Randall got his money back after he shot Rantwon in the head. Randall will now enjoy the company of a whole new set of gambling buddies for the next twenty years to life.

Tim Eves of England, a twenty-five-year-old scout leader who enjoyed cycling, fishing, and other healthy outdoor activities, was pronounced dead on arrival at a local hospital in March 2009. His girlfriend, Emma Tuck, and their friend Lewis Hickin tried unsuccessfully to revive Eves when he collapsed shortly after playing the Nintendo game Wii Fit.

Saad Khan, a thirty-two-year-old contestant on a Pakistani *Survivor*-style reality show, had already been eliminated from the show but was called back in August 2009 for one more chance to make it to the show's finals. The special challenge consisted of swimming across a murky Bangkok lake carrying fifteen pounds of gear.

In the middle of the swim, Khan called out once and went under. Fellow contestants and other members of the show's crew immediately jumped into the lake to try to rescue him but were unsuccessful. Divers later found the body. Khan was returned to his hometown of Karachi. The show's sponsor, Unilever Pakistan, accepted no liability for the death. Spokespeople indicated that this particular episode probably wouldn't air. Unilever was reconsidering its plans to continue sponsoring the show.

A freak thunderstorm broke out over a rugby game in Annapolis, Maryland, in the summer of 2000. Donald Patton, one of the spectators, and several other people ran for cover. Their mistake was in seeking shelter under some trees. Donald, six rugby players, and two other spectators were zapped to death when a massive lightning bolt struck their tree.

Barry Buckingham, a forty-four-year-old window cleaner from Peterborough, England, was a serious darts fan who played in a league called the New England Club without fail every Monday night and attended matches at least twice a week—until, that is, he said he felt a bit warm while celebrating his team's victory over the Post Office Club in July 2007 and promptly dropped dead. "He died doing what he loved," said former teammate Phil Green, which might have been true if he had been killed by a dart.

$\clubsuit$

Everybody loved Skeeter Johnston, and Skeeter Johnston loved polo. He was participating in a practice game at the family farm near the Florida Everglades in April 2007 when he fell off his horse. It was not the first time he had fallen off a horse, and he did, in fact, survive the fall. It was the trampling that killed him.

$\clubsuit$

Thomas Junta was upset that his son was being unnecessarily roughed up by another kid during hockey practice in Reading, Massachusetts, in July 2000. To make his point, the 275-pound Junta approached Michael Costin, the father of the purported bully, and beat the man to death. Junta is now serving six to ten years in prison.

Malcolm Baldrige was the U.S. secretary of commerce during the Reagan administration. He was also a member of the Rodeo Cowboys Association and good enough at the sport to win prize money from time to time. He was even inducted into the Cowboy Hall of Fame in 1984.

In the summer of 1987, while participating in a rodeo in California, Baldrige was crushed when his horse fell on him.

Geoff Neely from Sydney, Australia, was taking glider piloting lessons at the Lake Keepit Soaring Club in New South Wales in February 2007. The glider was connected to a propeller plane by a two-hundred-foot cable.

Both planes got off the ground successfully, but the pilot of the propeller plane noticed that the cable was about to become entangled in a row of trees at the end of the runway. He released the cable from his plane and trusted that the instructor in the glider would guide the student to a safe landing.

The propeller plane landed back on the runway, but the glider slammed into a wire fence, which permanently separated the trainee, Geoff, from his head. The instructor walked away with a few minor scratches.

🐟

Retired cop and high school assistant Dennin Bauers of Minnesota loved hockey with a passion. His dedication to the game drove him to personally inspect the ice every morning at the Duluth Entertainment Convention Center, where he coached his sons and other kids every evening after work. Bauers was also a careful man; he wore a helmet when he played. Sadly, the wild hockey puck that killed him during a practice game in 2006 hit him right behind the ear, just below the helmet.

🐟

By all accounts, up-and-coming varsity football star Joseph Cardella was a great athlete, but not such a good driver. He flipped his all-terrain vehicle while riding in a vacant lot next to his Ingleside, Illinois, home in August 2008 and landed on his head. He arrived at the hospital DOA.

Jiang Tao was the SinChi Football Club's tallest soccer player. Team manager Wang Jinhui said this was probably why it was Jiang and no other players who was struck by lightning during a March 2004 training session.

During a Calgary Flames vs. Blue Jackets hockey game in Columbus, Ohio, in 2002, Epsen Knutsen hit the puck with such force that it flew over the glass at the far end of the rink, bounced off a spectator, and hit thirteen-year-old Brittanie Cecil in the head. The incident is believed to be the first time a spectator was killed by a puck during a National Hockey League game. Most spectators who are killed by pucks die in minor league and amateur games.

On the evening of England's loss to Portugal in the Euro 2004 soccer games, several brawls broke out among a group of South Wales railroad workers staying at the Cricketers Arms guesthouse in Banbury, Oxfordshire. Kevin Lavelle was involved in all of them. The twenty-nine-year-old crane operator received more than fifty blows before the dust had finally settled for the evening, including not just one but two blows to the head with an iron dumbbell bar. It was the last one that probably killed him.

There had been so many separate scuffles, all of them violent, so many injuries to the victims, and not a single consistent story from the other men involved in the fights that the coroner would not confirm anything but that Lavelle was dead.

The destinies of Chucky Mullins and Curtis Williams seemed to have been preordained by supernatural forces. Both were defensive backs on their respective college football teams (University of Mississippi and University of Washington). Both tackled the fullbacks on the opposing teams (Vanderbilt and Stanford, respectively). Both plays resulted in the same spine-shattering injury: permanent paralysis. Both men were injured on the same day—October 28. Both died eighteen months after being injured. Both died on the same day—May 6. The men had never met one another. Their injuries and deaths occurred exactly eleven years apart. Mullins died in 1989, and Williams in 2000.

Ken Costin, a thirty-nine-year-old metalworker from Sandy, Bedfordshire, in the UK, is believed to be the first person killed during a game of paintball. While playing the game in the fall of 2001, he was crouched behind a hay bale when an opponent approached from the rear. Costin was wearing a protective mask, but the paintball hit him in the back of the head. He died ten days later.

Mark Goodkey, a twenty-two-year-old hockey player with the University of Alberta Golden Bears, dived onto the ice to block a slap shot in the third quarter of a March 1996 game. The hockey puck hit him in the neck, killing him instantly.

During a 2001 soccer game between Persepolis and Shemooshak at Mottaqi Stadium in Iran, a few of the spectators climbed atop the partially constructed roof to get a better view. The structure collapsed during the second half of the game, causing people and debris to come crashing onto the heads of those in the stands below.

As police and rescue workers arrived to render aid, twenty thousand spectators—from the panic-stricken to the hyper-violent—began dismantling the arena, mostly with their bare hands. They tore down one of the stadium walls, ripped iron fences out of the ground, attacked antiriot police with rocks and poles, and, inexplicably, set several fires on the field. Some of the players took refuge in the locker rooms and were trapped there for hours. One was hit in the head with a rock as he tried to flee the field.

Of those in attendance that day, dozens were killed and hundreds were injured—a few as a result of the roof collapse, and the rest by the crazed mob composed mostly of people who were apparently unfamiliar with the terms "orderly exit" and "assigned seating."

Kostydin Yankov, a promising biochemistry undergraduate student at Oxford University in England, was a member of the Oxford Stunt Factory, the school's extreme sports club. At an exhibition in 2005, members of the club dressed in elaborate costumes and prepared to put on a big show. A catapult was designed in the style of a trebuchet, the kind favored by the ancient Romans for hurling large boulders and disease-infested corpses over the walls of their enemies' castles.

Kostydin got into the specially made catapult and was shot a hundred feet into the air—missing the safety net completely. He died of extreme injuries.

🐛

Doctors had warned Tony Morabito, owner of the San Francisco 49ers, that the stress and emotion inherent to the game of football would probably kill him. Sure enough, it did. Morabito dropped dead of a heart attack in the stands at halftime during a game against the Chicago Bears on October 27, 1957.

🐛

In January 2006, Mark Cawthrow from Barnesley, England, took his girlfriend, Fiona, to the beautiful Spanish island of Ibiza to celebrate their fifth anniversary. While there, he decided to take a paragliding lesson. An instructor took him on a fifteen-minute tandem flight, towed by a boat called *Take Off the Second*. The flight was a spectacular experience for the happy thirty-four-year-old, as everyone heard him say while he and his instructor made a perfect landing.

When the instructor went to remove the harness attached to Mark's safety bar and parachute, the wind suddenly dropped, sending the parachute into the water. The weight of the water in the parachute put such an enormous strain on the rope that it snapped, which sent the metal hand bar slamming into Mark's midsection. The impact ruptured Mark's spleen and caused massive internal injuries. The coroner ruled Mark's death a terrible freak accident.

It was Mark and Fiona's first (and only) trip to a foreign country.

On October 25, 1998, the impossible happened: All eleven players of Congo's Bena Tshadi soccer team were killed when they were struck by lightning during a game. Thirty more people, mostly spectators on the sidelines, were injured. However, not a single member of the opposing team was harmed.

Unable to produce a logical explanation for what was truly inexplicable, investigators blamed the freak occurrence on witchcraft. To the people of that village, this seemed a perfectly acceptable explanation, as good as any they'd ever gotten before from anyone in authority.

Unlucky Stiffs

Vincent Tan, a seventeen-year-old from Singapore, had attained a green belt in tae kwon do in just one year of training. He felt utterly prepared for some real competition, so he signed up for a match at the Kampong Kembangan Community Club in July 2009.

Vincent was paired with a younger competitor who had achieved the slightly higher ranking of brown belt. Organizers seemed to believe that the size and age difference between the boys would compensate for the disparity in skill level. They were wrong. The younger competitor dealt Vincent a powerful kick to the neck. Vincent adjusted his headgear, then fell to the floor, brain-dead. A few days later, he was pronounced completely dead.

The unnamed young man with the deadly kick showed up at Vincent's funeral to pay his respects and formally apologize to his mother, Madam Nur Julia. She screamed insults and obscenities at him. He took it like a man but will probably not compete in any more tae kwon do matches.

While jogging in a Philadelphia park in August 2009, an unidentified woman was killed instantly when a thirty-foot tree branch fell on her head. Police say she probably never knew what hit her; she was wearing earphones connected to her portable music player when the branch came crashing down. There's something to be said about the endurance of some of these portable devices, though. The music was still playing when they pried the tree limb off her.

❧

Two teenage skateboarders were practicing their moves on a sidewalk near their home in Plymouth, England, in April 2007. One of them lost his balance, which sent the skateboard skittering off the curb and into the street. When he went to retrieve it, he didn't see forty-seven-year-old Tim Honey, who was traveling along the road on his Suzuki motorcycle at a perfectly legal rate of speed. Honey's bike struck the teenager and then swerved to the other side of the road. Honey was killed by a car traveling in the other direction. The skateboarders and the driver of the car survived.

❧

Derek Batten and brothers John and Peter Tunstead set off on a great Australian adventure in early April 2007. The men, ages fifty-nine, sixty-three, and sixty-nine, respectively, planned to journey from Queensland to Perth on a thirty-two-foot catama-ran, a trip they estimated would take six to eight weeks.

On April 18, the *Kaz II* was found drifting off the northern Australian coast. Forensic scientists pieced together what had happened to the three amigos.

One of the Tunstead brothers fell into the water when he tried to free a fishing line from the boat's propeller. The other brother fell in when he tried to save him.

Derek, the only experienced sailor in the bunch, then ad-justed the sails to turn the boat around to rescue Peter and John. The wind suddenly shifted direction, causing the yacht's boom to swing around and knock Derek overboard, which tore the sail. Once all three were in the water, the *Kaz II* sailed away without them.

Sixty-nine-year-old Harvey Taylor from Canterbury, New Zea-land, was an enthusiastic jet boat salesman for thirty-five years before starting his own business as a fishing guide. The fact that he had lost an arm in an accident fifty years before never kept him from his love of boating and adventure.

On October 31, 2004, Harvey was on a recreational trip with friends on the Waimakariri River when the steering on his fourteen-foot boat suddenly failed. The oar he was using to control the boat slammed into his midsection, causing massive internal injuries. The boat then drifted downstream and finally collided with three bluffs. By the time rescue workers arrived, Harvey was dead.

Conditions on the river that day were vexingly ordinary.

🪱

Just for fun, Corporal Andrew Thompson from Holmfield, Halifax, in the UK was participating in a shooting competition at a Territorial Army training ground near Catterick Garrison in North Yorkshire on April 15, 2000. As he pulled the trigger on his 9mm pistol, the weapon suddenly exploded in his hand. One bullet traveled backward and hit him in the head and neck. Commander Brigadier Alan Deed said, "We rarely have accidents with pistols." The military much prefers that guns be used to kill people on purpose.

🪱

In September 2006, Neil Powers, a forty-three-year-old man from Coventry, England who played for the Pinley Rugby Club, got into an argument with game officials over a "scrum" (restarting the game after the ball has accidentally gone out of play). Powers suddenly dropped dead on the field, right in the middle of the argument. Ironically, the game was being played in memory of Alan Tucker, who played on a team called Coventry Tech and had died two years earlier.

Placed in the awkward position of figuring out how best to honor Alan Tucker in future games, Coventry Tech decided a nice trophy would be better than organizing another memorial match.

The headquarters of the Long Mynd Gliding Club was near a popular nature preserve in Shropshire, England. The location was especially welcoming to hikers, horseback riders, and other nature lovers.

In the summer of 1998, Muriel Jones, a sixty-six-year-old widow who had recently moved to the area, was enjoying a peaceful late-evening walk through the quiet fields. Just then, forty-nine-year-old Michael Woolley was making a silent descent in his glider. The plane hit Jones, killing her instantly.

❧

Noncho Vodenicharov, the fifty-three-year-old mayor of a small town in Bulgaria and a former stuntman, was competing in a *Survivor*-style reality show in the Camarines Sur province of the Philippines when he dropped dead of a heart attack in the middle of a challenge.

❧

Crosty View and Woodbrook Jo, two greyhounds headed for the 2003 Kent Derby dog races in England, were let off their leads by their trainer early one morning for a romp in the fields, a pee, and whatever other personal business needed tending after a long night in the kennels. The dogs set off in their usual insanely happy way, galloping merrily through the dewy grass at full speed. They crashed into each other head-on, hit a tree, and fell down dead. Both of them.

❧

Sean Haughey, a teenager from Wales, was a huge fan of the MTV program *Jackass*. The show runs explicit warnings with every episode, reminding viewers that the stars of the show are *professional* jackasses and that the folks at home should not try any of the sick pranks, disgusting shenanigans, or dangerous stunts they've just seen. As if that ever stopped anyone.

Sean was one of those viewers for whom such warnings might as well have been written in hieroglyphics. He tried duplicating many of the stunts he saw on the show, including doing a back-flip off a wall, which almost put him in traction. In August 2007, Sean's parents came home to find him dead in the backyard with a broken neck. They didn't wonder how it happened.

On a gloriously sunny day in the summer of 2003, Jamie Morgan went fishing with a friend in the Rhymney River in the tiny village of Hengoed, Wales. They chose a spot near the Maesycwmmer viaduct, which is known to have fast-moving whirlpools and deep underwater crevices. The fish seemed to like it.

Jamie's waders filled up with water almost as soon as he stepped into the river, and the currents quickly carried him away. Rescue workers wearing special gear found him downriver a couple hours later, completely waterlogged and having given new meaning to the notion of dying with one's boots on.

UPS retiree Sam White got hooked on scavenging and collecting Civil War artifacts when he was a boy growing up in Virginia. It would become a lifelong avocation.

On February 18, 2008, Sam had eighteen cannonballs all lined up in his driveway. He frequently restored such unearthed finds for other collectors and museums. Restoration usually involved disarming these seventy-five-pound, nine-inch explosive spheres, and then using a power drill attached to a grinder to remove a century and a half of grit, rust, and dirt. The shower of sparks is believed to have set off the particular cannonball that killed him. The explosion also sent shrapnel through the front porch of a house a quarter-mile away.

In October 2001, when British police officer Andrew Rennie failed to show up for his shift, fellow officers went to his house in Stechford, Birmingham. They found him dangling from the ceiling of his bedroom, wrapped in a convoluted system of ropes and pulleys, dressed in women's clothing, and wearing a stylishly feminine wig. Andrew had become hopelessly entangled in his own contraption and had suffocated in his attempt at autoerotic stimulation.

His wife, Ann-Marie, who had gone away for the weekend with a girlfriend, flew back home immediately upon hearing the news. She told officers that when her husband had dropped her off at the train station the Friday before, he had seemed perfectly normal. The notion of her husband in drag came as a complete shock.

Of the very few people for whom it can rightfully be said, "He died doing something he loved," David Carradine is most certainly near the top of the list. The seventy-two-year-old actor, best known for his role as Caine (or by the affectionate nickname "Grasshopper") in the 1970s television drama *Kung Fu* and as Bill in the *Kill Bill* movies, probably never intended to exit this life naked and strangled, but his last thoughts were almost certainly very happy ones.

Some of Carradine's ex-wives told the press that our beloved "Grasshopper" was adept at self-bondage. On June 3, 2009, Carradine was found dead in the closet of his hotel room in Bangkok, Thailand. His hands were tied, but there was no sign or evidence that anyone but Carradine had been in the room before or after his death, a fact supported by the ex-wives' claims.

Except for a shoelace tied around his penis and a rope around his neck, Carradine was naked.

After examining the body, authorities determined the death to be a tragic case of accidental autoerotic asphyxia.

The *New York Post* reported the news under the headline, "Hung Fu." Remarkably, this was in better taste than the Thai newspapers' reportage. One paper published a picture of the dead actor on its front page. Another published the actual autopsy photos.

6

CURED TO DEATH

Some years ago, I came down with the worst cold or flu (I can never tell the difference) I'd ever experienced in my life. A friend stopped by to check on me, to see if it was time for an ambulance or a hearse. I would have nothing to do with either, and if I had been able to speak, I would have told her so.

She either read the look in my crossed eyes or figured it out on her own, but she decided it was probably best not to move me. "I'll make you a cup of tea," she said. I smiled, or grimaced, or groaned, or something. It was the best I could do by way of an expression of gratitude.

As I waited for the sound of the teakettle, I could almost taste the Lipton's or chamomile I kept in my cupboard. Just thinking about it made me feel better.

My friend came back with a concoction so vile I can barely summon the words to describe it. It was the color of nothing I had ever seen in nature or in nightmares. There was dark smoke—not white steam—rising in weird curls from the large cup. And the smell ... oh, that smell. There was even a chunk of something swimming at the bottom. I made a noise that sounded like a moose call.

"Good," she said, "it's working already. You've regained your ability to whine. Now roll over so I can plaster some of this on your back. The tea will be ready in a minute."

Sometimes the cure is worse than the malady. Sometimes the cure *is* the malady. I was lucky my friend wasn't trained in the curative arts by any of the people in the following stories.

Mohamed Kader Mydin and his wife, Rosina Mydin Pillay, visited their nephew Ibrahim in Kuala Lumpur, Malaysia, in October 2008 after hearing that the young man had learned some new healing techniques through his association with a nontraditional religious sect. Mohamed wanted to quit smoking; Rosina had a liver ailment. Ibrahim was overjoyed at the prospect of helping his aunt and uncle.

With the aid of three other male relatives who were also well-versed in the healing ritual, Ibrahim smashed Mohamed's and Rosina's heads against a table and then beat them with broomsticks and motorcycle helmets. When Mohamed and Rosina failed to regain consciousness after several hours, the healers called an ambulance. Mohamed and Rosina were pronounced dead at the scene.

Andrew Stewart, a high school student from Dunfermline, Scotland, dreamed of a future as a firefighter. In the meantime, he was a star hockey player on his school's team. He was the very picture of youthful health and vigor until he had to be substituted in a game in 2006 because of an inexplicable loss of energy. He was admitted to the hospital and diagnosed with lymphoblastic leukemia. While undergoing chemotherapy, he fell victim to necrotizing fasciitis, a flesh-eating bacteria. Two weeks later, he was dead.

In October 2009, self-help expert James Arthur Ray conducted a five-day workshop called "Spiritual Warrior" at the Angel Valley Spiritual Retreat in Arizona. People paid $9,650 a head for the privilege of "retreating from the bus-i-ness of life" and participating in a series of mind-body exercises designed to create mental, physical, and financial wellness. One of these exercises was a variation on an ancient Native American practice known as the sweat lodge, a sort of ceremonial sauna conducted in a darkened hut or tent. It is designed to purify the mind, body, and spirit, and typically lasts about an hour.

On the day before the scheduled conclusion of Ray's workshop, the sixty or so participants were sent on a thirty-six-hour "cleansing" fast—no food *or* water—through the desert. Afterward, handlers ushered them to the retreat center and gave them a snack. Just when they thought the fun was all over, Ray announced that he had one more surprise for them. He led them to a roasting-hot, pitch-dark, 415-square-foot tent for what he called "a sweat lodge experience."

Within minutes, people began vomiting and passing out. Ray insisted they all fight the urge to leave, that this experience would make them stronger. All it did was make them sicker and, in some cases, dead.

After two hours in the makeshift enclosure, more than twenty participants were finally taken to local hospitals for treatment, some with multiple organ failure. James Shore and Kirby Brown died that night. Liz Neuman, who was in excellent physical condition before attending the retreat, died two weeks later without ever coming out of her coma.

Shortly after news of the debacle got out, Ray posted a Twitter message saying, "... for anything new to live something first must die."

It does not appear that tact and sensitivity are traits that figure prominently in Ray's vision of spiritual wealth.

Mary McClinton, a sixty-nine-year-old Seattle-area resident, visited the Virginia Mason Medical Center to take care of a small problem with her eyes. What ensued was one of the most horrific deaths in the history of hospital care.

While she was sitting in the waiting room on the day of her eye appointment in the late summer of 2004, a large picture fell off the wall and hit her on the head. Still dizzy after a few days, she went with her son to a different hospital, where a brain scan revealed that she had an aneurysm.

McClinton returned to Virginia Mason for X-rays to help doctors locate and treat the aneurysm. The procedure required the use of a dye that would make the aneurysm more visible on the films. But instead of the dye, a nurse accidentally injected a toxic cleaning solution directly into one of McClinton's arteries.

The chemical damage to McClinton's blood vessels blocked the flow of blood to the muscles in her leg, causing extremely painful swelling. The doctors decided that the best way to stop the pain in her leg was to chop it off. That didn't even come close to solving the problem of toxic chemicals flowing through her veins. Kidney failure came next, and then a sudden drop in blood pressure, followed by the stroke that finally killed her.

The original eye problem was never a life-threatening condition.

Elaine Bromiley, an otherwise healthy thirty-seven-year-old British mother of two, had suffered for years from sinusitis. Her doctor recommended a surgical procedure to straighten the inside of her nose, which could stop the recurrence of sinusitis and prevent possible damage to the optic nerve.

While she was sedated, Elaine's airway collapsed, blocking the flow of oxygen to her brain. The surgical team went to work immediately to get a breathing tube down her throat. A nurse called the ICU to see if a bed was available. A second nurse got a tracheotomy tray in case the breathing-tube trick didn't work.

The surgical staff were so intent on doing their job—inserting the breathing tube—that they didn't notice that more than half an hour had passed before they succeeded. The nurses were perfectly capable of performing the tracheotomy that could have saved Elaine's life, but as "junior staff" they deferred to the doctors and decided not to speak up, thinking the doctors would not have listened to them anyway. The net effect was that Bromiley died of an extreme case of "Don't look at me. I just work here."

In September 2008, forty-five-year-old Brian Sinclair waited thirty-four hours in the emergency room of the Winnipeg Health Sciences Centre, propped up in a wheelchair. Hospital security staff spoke to him, and housekeepers cleaned around him. He was a "regular" at the hospital, and staff knew him well. But not a single nurse or clinician through four or five shifts stopped to ask how he was doing that day or why he was there. It was a fellow emergency room patient who noticed he was dead.

Nearly everyone in Rev. Richard Coley's former congregation at Victoria Tollcross Church in Glasgow, Scotland, believed he only meant to alleviate the suffering of his frail seventy-one-year-old wife, Isabella. She had undergone heart surgery in 2001 and was entering an advanced stage of dementia.

One summer night in 2007, Coley gave his wife of forty-six years a few extra sleeping pills. As the evening wore on and Isabella continued to breathe, he began to fear he had not given her enough of the sedative to kill her. So he stabbed her in the back.

Isabella was not as frail as she looked. She lay bleeding on their bed but showed no signs of giving up the ghost anytime soon. So the good reverend lifted her arm and stabbed her in the side to be sure to pierce her heart.

Coley then went to the bathroom, stood over the sink, turned on the hot water, and prepared to slit his own wrists. To his horror, Isabella suddenly stumbled in, dazed and bleeding, looking somewhat confused but very much alive. She asked him what was going on.

Coley made one last attempt on Isabella's life. He strangled her until he was sure she was dead. He then returned to the business of slitting his own wrists.

The couple's daughter discovered the grisly scene and called for help. Coley was taken to a mental hospital and was released a few months later. When he got home, he posted notes on his windows telling the neighbors to contact the police. Then he hanged himself.

While many people continue to believe the reverend's mercy-killing version of the story, some remain skeptical. He never explained why he had meticulously transferred all of his wife's money and assets out of her name just days before he killed her.

❧

A mere three months after the world-renowned Duke University Medical Center kicked off its first Patient Safety Week in 1994, experienced cardiac surgeon James Jaggers successfully completed a heart and lung transplant on seventeen-year-old Yésica Santillán. He forgot to check the blood type before the surgery, though, which turned out to be incompatible with Yésica's. As they were sewing her back up, her own body began to attack the donated organs. She was dead within hours.

The girl's family was understandably distraught over the outcome, but Yésica's mother flew into a full-blown rage when the staff at Duke had the presence of mind to ask whether it would be okay to take back the heart and lungs now that Yésica didn't need them anymore.

⁂

James Michael had been married to a former University of West Virginia cheerleader for five years when things took a tragic turn. Michelle Michael, now a pediatric nurse practitioner, was having an affair with one of James's employees. She also had very expensive tastes. So on the night of November 29, 2005, she injected James with a lethal dose of a paralyzing drug, then left him on the bed they had shared as husband and wife, while she went about setting their Morgantown, West Virginia, house on fire. There was also the very tempting matter of James's $500,000 life insurance policy.

Michelle is now serving a life sentence at the Lakin Correctional Center.

⁂

Heather Allen of Uniontown, Pennsylvania, was being prepped for arthroscopic surgery to remove a cyst in her shoulder. The procedure required injecting adrenaline (or epinephrine) into the joint, which would cause it to expand enough for the surgeon to insert a viewing instrument. Instead of Heather's joint, the adrenaline was inadvertently injected into a vein. Within seconds, Heather's heart began to race, then it stopped cold.

Incredibly, the state's chief medical examiner, James Kaplan, was quoted as saying, "It was just a freak occurrence. In my view, it seems like everything was done correctly."

Kathleen Grundy, a wealthy eighty-one-year-old woman who was once the mayor of Hyde, England, adored her doctor, Harold Shipman. The sweet, gentle physician made house calls and everything. Still when Grundy died on June 24, 1998, and left her entire estate to Dr. Shipman, her family became suspicious. There was something about the sloppily typed will that didn't look right, either.

Grundy's daughter, Angela, asked to have her mother's body exhumed. The medical examiner found that Grundy had died of a lethal dose of diamorphine, the clinical name for heroin.

The friends and families of a lot of other old ladies who adored Dr. Shipman came forward when they heard the news. Authorities began disinterring bodies left and right. To everyone's horror, it quickly became apparent that Dr. Shipman had been busy practicing his special form of medicine for a very long time.

There was enough diamorphine stashed in Dr. Shipman's house for 1,500 fatal doses. He had been writing fake prescriptions and stockpiling the drug for years, and helping himself to whatever money he could pilfer from the estates of countless widows, spinsters, and lonely old souls who thought they had hit the jackpot with such a personally attentive physician.

Dr. Shipman is believed to be responsible for the deaths of as many as 250 women who placed their trust and their lives in the hands of their friendly neighborhood family physician. He was convicted in February 2000 for fifteen of those murders.

🐛

Dr. John Baksh, a resident of London, England, was not a particularly warm human being. He ruled his home with an iron fist and terrorized everyone in his general vicinity with his dictatorial style. So, while on vacation in Spain on New Year's Eve 1982, no one was more surprised than Ruby, his wife of twenty-one years, when, in an uncharacteristic moment of tenderness, he brought her a cup of warm milk to help her sleep. An hour later, Ruby slept deeply indeed, thanks to the huge dose of sleeping pills Dr. Baksh had crushed into the milk. But not deeply enough, thought Dr. Baksh. So he injected her with a fatal dose of morphine. Because he was a respected physician, no one questioned Dr. Baksh's assertion that his wife had died of a sudden heart attack.

Seven days later, he married the beautiful Mahdu, a junior partner in his medical practice. They had a lovely fake Hindu wedding, and he gave Mahdu his dead wife's wedding ring. While on their fake honeymoon, Dr. Baksh told his new sort-of wife, "I sacrificed Ruby for you."

Mahdu was too terrified to do anything with this information. She endured sleeping next to a confessed murderer for years. The tension between them grew, along with Mahdu's depression. So, to cheer her up, one night in January 1986, Dr. Baksh poured his sad wife a glass of champagne, mixed with a healthy dose of the same kind of sleeping pills he had given to his first wife, followed by a booster shot of morphine. And to keep from making the circumstances seem too similar to his first murder, he drove her to a nature preserve, placed her under a holly bush, and slit Mahdu's throat.

By chance, a naturalist looking for toads found Mahdu. She was still alive.

Weeks later, still in the hospital but having recovered sufficient strength to write a note, she told police, "My husband is a killer. He killed his first wife."

Paul Vickers of Newcastle, England, was a successful orthopedic surgeon who aspired to a political career in Parliament. He also had a crippling inferiority complex when it came to women. At the root of this problem, it was said, was his crazy mother.

Dr. Vickers was most comfortable around emotionally disturbed and physically disabled women. His wife, Margaret, was an invalid. However, in the mid-1970s, Dr. Vickers became smitten with a former beauty queen named Pamela Collinson. The two began a torrid affair, which Pamela was certain would culminate in her becoming the doctor's second wife. Dr. Vickers, however, had been advised that a divorce would hurt his political career, so he injected his depressed and housebound wife with a cancer-fighting drug that induced a leukemia-like anemia. Within weeks, Margaret was dead.

Pamela the mistress waited a few months before pressing Dr. Vickers again about getting married. When he refused, Pamela suddenly discovered she had a conscience. She gathered a bunch of fake prescriptions for the same kind of drug that had killed Margaret, which Dr. Vickers had written for her friends and colleagues, and delivered the evidence to the police.

In 1981, Dr. Vickers was convicted of murder and sentenced to life in prison.

A homeless man named Ellis Greene arrived at the office of Dr. Richard Boggs, a wealthy Glendale, California, neurosurgeon, one fine day in 1988. Among other things, Ellis was drunk out of his mind. Dr. Boggs easily knocked him out with a stun gun and then suffocated him. He told police Ellis died of a heart attack.

It was soon discovered that Dr. Boggs and a couple of his best buddies had come up with the perfect insurance scam. They had asked Dr. Boggs to order them a $50,000 medical cadaver and then pass the body off as that of Melvin Hanson, one of the buddies. Hanson had a million-dollar life insurance policy. Dr. Boggs was supposed to plant Hanson's wallet and ID on the corpse—which he did, only the corpse was not a $50,000 medical cadaver. It was Greene, the drunk bum he brought in from the streets.

Dr. Boggs is serving a life sentence for insurance fraud and murder.

Hanson was arrested in 1991 as he got off a plane returning home from a vacation in Acapulco. In the intervening years, he had changed his name to Wolfgang Eugene von Snowden, had plastic surgery, and invested in hair transplants.

John Hawkins, the third buddy, was arrested off the coast of Sardinia at about the same time as Hanson, after his girlfriend heard of Hawkins's infidelities on *The Oprah Winfrey Show* and turned him in to the police.

In 1846, Dr. William Palmer rented a house in his hometown of Rugeley in Staffordshire, England, hung his shingle, and settled into a nice little life as a general practitioner with his wife, the former Annie Brookes. For fun, he gambled away nearly every cent he ever had on horse races. The shortage of cash was so severe that he often fretted that he and Annie couldn't afford to have children. To his great relief, four of his five children died within a few weeks of being born. A sixth child, which he had with his mistress, also died quite unexpectedly after one of Dr. Palmer's visits.

Dr. Palmer tried to talk his wealthy mother-in-law into stopping by for a visit, to which she replied, "I know I shall not live a fortnight!" She finally gave in and showed up, and died of a purported apoplectic fit just a few days later.

Many other relatives, especially the rich ones, had a nasty habit of dropping dead after visiting the Palmers. One who survived was an elderly aunt who became ill quite suddenly during one such family visit. Palmer gave her some pills, which she threw out the window as soon as she got home. When she went out to her yard the next morning, it was littered with dead chickens.

In 1854, a month or so after Dr. Palmer took out a huge life insurance policy on his wife, Annie Palmer died in a massive explosion of diarrhea. Amazingly, Dr. Palmer's brother Walter died in exactly the same manner, with Dr. Palmer named as the beneficiary of the life insurance policy. Suspecting foul play, the insurer refused to pay on the second policy. They demanded that Walter's body be exhumed and examined. The cause of death could not be determined because Walter's body exploded as soon as they opened his coffin.

Dr. Palmer was hanged in 1856 for the last person he killed, a fellow horse racing enthusiast who accompanied the doctor home for a brandy after a particularly lucky day at the track. John Parsons Cook soon fell ill, so Dr. Palmer gave him a shot of morphine and served him a cup of beef broth laced with strychnine.

Dr. Palmer's little house in Rugeley still stands on Market Street. It is a popular tourist attraction.

&

All four of Dr. Robert George Clements's wives preceded him in death. The first one died of sleeping sickness in 1920. The second died of endocarditis (an inflammation of the inner layer of the heart) in 1925. Wife number three died of cancer in 1939. His last wife died of leukemia in 1947. All but the third wife were very wealthy women. All four were penniless at the times of their deaths. All four death certificates were signed by Dr. Clements.

Eventually authorities in Southport, England, could no longer ignore the outrage and suspicions of the town's citizens. Police arrived at Dr. Clements's home and found him already dead. They also found a suicide note stating, "I can no longer tolerate the diabolical insults to which I have been recently exposed."

꙳

A man from the southern province of Hainan in China became suspicious of a bottle of mineral water when the member of his family who had been drinking from it suddenly began to vomit blood. He fed the rest of the water to one of his chickens, just to make sure. In less than a minute, the chicken was dead.

Beijing News reported this story in September 2007, raising additional concerns over the safety and quality of goods made in China. The item included a picture of the man holding the plastic bottle and squatting next to the dead chicken.

It should come as some relief to those Americans who are convinced that China is trying to kill us with dangerously tainted products. The Chinese are scared, too.

❧

Seventy-three-year-old Hazel Grey had just been discharged from the James Cook University Hospital in Middlesbrough, England, in 2008. In a wheelchair, she was slowly making her way out of one of the hospital elevators with her husband, who also was using a wheelchair, rolling out just ahead of her. When Mr. Grey turned to check on his wife's progress, all he saw was Hazel's one remaining leg sticking out of the doors. She was screaming, in a panic because the doors were clamped tight around her leg and the rest of her was still inside the lift.

Hazel was eventually rescued from the killer elevator, but by then the damage had been done. The injury caused a blood clot that doctors said would disappear over time. It did not. Instead, she developed blood poisoning, which got into her brain and heart and killed her in a few short days.

In the 1700s, medical practitioners believed that insufflation, or the act of blowing air into the body, had the power to resuscitate the nearly dead. It was also a good way to verify that a person was really dead before committing mortal remains to the earth forever.

The practice is believed to have started in the eighteenth century. The Royal Humane Society of England reported that in 1746, an unconscious woman was pulled from the water near London. A sailor who was passing by suggested that someone blow air into the woman's body. One of the rescuers asked the sailor to lend him his pipe, and the sailor obliged. The rescuer then inserted the stem of the pipe in the woman's rectum, and blew into the bowl of the pipe. Miraculously, the half-drowned woman came back to life.

Convinced they had found a cure for drowning, the Royal Humane Society of England began installing smoke enema kits at intervals along the Thames River. Medical practitioners believed that part of what had saved the woman was the tobacco smoke in the sailor's pipe.

But this form of insufflation actually killed more people than it saved. By the 1900s, medical science finally figured out that it was far more effective to blow regular air into a "nearly dead" person's lungs than to force tobacco smoke up their asses.

7

I LOVE YOU TO PIECES

It is said that every person is capable of seeing the fatal flaw in his or her significant other from the very first moments of a new relationship. The problem is that the sickness known as "love" has a funny way of blinding us to those important clues. And it's all kinds of love that can do a person in—romantic love, love of money and social status, and love of danger masquerading as excitement or adventure, to name a few.

What I wonder is this: How blind does a person have to be to get involved with a homicidal maniac? And wouldn't some of those clues manifest themselves in some glaring way sometime between the first date and the trip down the aisle?

I once dumped a guy after two dates because he gesticulated so wildly when he spoke that he almost put my eye out with his dinner fork while he was telling me about his day. But maybe that's just me. Maybe I overreacted. Maybe I judged him unfairly. Or maybe I saved myself from a serious head injury and possible permanent disfigurement. Who's to say with any certainty?

Then there are those whose relationships are purely coincidental: siblings, parents, offspring, cousins, aunts, and uncles. I firmly believe that one's closest relatives should live at least three hours away. By plane.

What follows here are stories of people who, if not for their loved ones, might have lived long enough to die from something perfectly natural, like a mudslide or a shark attack.

Timothy Wayne Shepherd went a bit overboard when he found out his ex-girlfriend Tynesha Stewart, a Texas A&M University freshman, had fallen in love with someone new while she was away at college. He confronted Stewart, and the encounter quickly escalated into a violent scuffle.

When Shepherd realized he had "accidentally" strangled Stewart, he put her in the bathtub, ran to the hardware store,

Unlucky Stiffs

and bought a jigsaw. Shepherd dismembered the poor girl and then attempted to dispose of the body parts by cooking them in a backyard barbecue pit. When neighbors complained about the smoke—which billowed for two straight days—Shepherd told them he was cooking for a wedding.

In October 2008, Shepherd was convicted of murder, sentenced to ninety-nine years in prison, and ordered to pay a fine in the amount of $10,000. Considering Texas has one of the highest rates of execution in the nation, he got off pretty easy.

❧

While visiting his cousins for a few days during the Christmas holiday in 1999, twenty-seven-year-old Mohammed Asrar of Birmingham, England, flew into a rage when his wife, Yasmin, announced that she no longer loved him. Mohammed said to her, "[But] I do love you and I'll prove it!" He ran into the kitchen, barricaded himself inside, and ransacked the knife drawer.

Yasmin had to enlist the help of her husband's cousin, Mohammed Jahangir, to break down the door. They found Yasmin's husband on the floor, covered in blood. He had stabbed himself in the liver and stomach, and opened a major artery.

Christopher Ball, the Birmingham deputy coroner, said that it was clear that Mohammed intended to stab himself, but he wasn't sure the man fully grasped that this particular demonstration of love could actually kill him.

❧

Twenty-three-year-old Gary Schuning from Addison, Illinois, evidently loved his mom. He said so on his MySpace page and posted pictures and blog entries to prove it. He loved her almost as much as he loved riding motorcycles, "partying with his peeps," and girls. But it was Mom, Doris Pagliaro, who was his personal hero. "I love her to death," he wrote. And he really meant it.

Police charge that Doris and her son got into an argument in March 2006 that culminated with him stabbing her to death. He then hid her body in their home, called an escort service, and ordered $1,200 worth of hookers for the evening. He allegedly used his mother's credit card to pay for these services.

Jesse Miser, the "escort coordinator," sent over twenty-one-year-old Kristi Hoenig. When Kristi discovered a bloody knife in the bathroom, she called her pimp in a panic. While she was on the phone, Gary stabbed and killed her, too.

Perhaps realizing that there was a potential witness still on the phone, Gary stabbed himself a few times to deflect any suspicions the authorities might have had about his being a double murderer.

Prosecutors are seeking the death penalty. Gary says he is innocent. Jesse the pimp, who cooperated fully with investigators, is serving four years in prison for pandering.

🐛

Despite the fact that he had had at least two extramarital affairs himself, thirty-two-year-old Sean Brooks of Brecon, Wales was crushed when the love of his life, Vicky Brooks, announced that she had fallen in love with a valet parking attendant she met at the gym. Sean followed his beautiful blond wife to her lover's house on the night of February 27, 2002, and forced his way inside. With the three of them standing in the kitchen, Sean tried to talk Vicky into coming back to him. To prove his love was true, he grabbed a knife from the counter and stabbed himself four times in the chest. His death was ruled a suicide.

🐛

Jonathan Donne and Michelle Harkett invited three of their junkie friends to their Swansea, Wales apartment on the evening of May 15, 2007. When Michelle refused to share the stash of heroin she had hidden in her vagina, Jonathan head-butted her. Michelle then made her way into the kitchen and emerged a few minutes later armed with a couple knives and a miniature samurai sword. She also had a pair of scissors sticking out of her thigh, where she had accidentally stabbed herself. Jonathan overpowered her and killed her with her own weapons. He then ran out of the building screaming, "Something has happened to my missus!"

Jonathan is serving four years for manslaughter.

As far as fifty-one-year-old Domenico Arico of Melbourne, Australia, was concerned, everything was in perfect order in his marriage—just the way he liked it—until his wife, Carmel, decided to take a class at a local university in 1996. Soon afterward, Domenico claimed that Carmel began to lose interest in her family and her wifely duties. She left without warning three years later and moved to Williamstown, about seven miles away. On May 10, 1999, somewhat bewildered and upset that his wife of twenty-five years had started a new life without him, he decided to pay her a visit.

Domenico confronted Carmel in the front yard of her new home. Words were exchanged, voices were raised, and fingers were wagged. One of those fingers was Domenico's, and it ended up in Carmel's mouth. She bit off a good chunk of the fourth finger of his left hand. So Domenico stabbed her forty-five times.

Domenico's lawyer told the court that Carmel would still be alive if she hadn't bitten him, and then proceeded to speak at great length about the extensive surgery poor Domenico had had to endure to repair his mutilated finger. It took the jury four hours to find him guilty of murder.

In June 2006, Adam Smith of Akron, Ohio, arrived home in the middle of the night to find his wife of seven months, Nicole Pantaleano, trying to kill herself with a knife. The sight so disturbed him that he took the knife away from her and stabbed her to death himself.

Ema Fiu, a twenty-seven-year-old bank teller living in Sydney, Australia, tried for two weeks to get her estranged boyfriend, Zoran Valsilevski, to come to see her. She made up stories and tried every trick in the book to convince him. On November 10,

1997, she finally succeeded. She hid a large kitchen knife under her bed and waited.

When Zoran arrived at her home, Ema begged him to take her back. He reiterated that he had broken up with her because of his parents' objections to their relationship. He allegedly told her she was good enough for sex, but not for marriage. Ema became hysterical. In an effort to comfort her, Zoran began performing oral sex on her. While he was thusly occupied, Ema stabbed him in the back and throat sixteen times.

Ema then tried to electrocute herself with a severed power cord, but failed. She went to jail instead.

🦎

Gavin James of Pretoria, South Africa, didn't let his use of a wheelchair keep him from living a full life. He had a girlfriend, Hendrika Coetzee, and often cooked dinner for her. They shared a home for eleven years and rented out a spare room to the occasional boarder.

Things were not always rosy, though. Hendrika and Gavin drank a lot. Money was always tight. Gavin once drove his wheelchair over Hendrika's foot because she was too slow in getting him out of the car. During another argument (no one could remember what it was about), he broke her thumb.

One night in October 2007, Gavin made Hendrika a plate of fried eggs for supper. They were not quite to her liking, so she stabbed him through the heart with her dinner knife.

Daniel Nel, the current boarder, found Gavin bleeding in the kitchen and Hendrika pouring herself another beer. She said she didn't see anybody stab her boyfriend.

Hendrika's lawyer convinced the court that the fried egg incident was merely the last item on a long list of Gavin's transgressions against her. Magistrate Kallie Bosch said, "Many women and men are beaten by their spouses in South Africa. The appeals court does not send them to jail." Hendrika got five years, but the sentence was unconditionally suspended as long as she stayed out of trouble during that period of time.

When forty-six-year-old Randall Fohr started dating a four-foot, eleven-inch hooker from Milwaukee named Mary Anntionette Rogers, his parents were less than pleased. They refused to let Randall bring her to their home. Randall continued seeing her anyway, even though she had been arrested several times between 1993 and 1997 on charges related to drugs and prostitution. However, in 1998, Randall finally decided to break things off.

They were sitting in a parked car when Randall gave Mary Anntionette the bad news. She flew into a rage. She produced a pair of scissors and jammed them into his chest. Then she pushed him out of the car and left.

A Good Samaritan who witnessed the altercation picked Randall up from the sidewalk and took him to the hospital, where he was pronounced dead. Randall's mother later explained that her son had never been very lucky in love.

❧

Catherine and Roger Osliffe were an affluent, well-educated couple in their mid-thirties living in Lancashire, England. She was a college lecturer who worked part-time counseling prison inmates on social and life skills; he was an entrepreneur in the fencing business.

On June 6, 2004, about a week after the couple returned from their honeymoon, Catherine's mother sent her some flowers. Roger, who had had quite a few drinks that evening, flew into a jealous rage, threw the flowers at her, and accused her of being involved with another man. Perhaps forgetting for a moment that she was something of an expert on teaching violent criminals how to live more harmoniously in society, Catherine ran to the kitchen, got a knife, and plunged it five inches into her husband's chest. She then waited ten minutes before calling for an ambulance.

When paramedics arrived, she told them Roger had stabbed himself. Roger raised his head briefly, gurgled, "Cath's done it," and got on with the business of bleeding to death.

Catherine got five years in jail.

☙

Marland Maynard of Stratford, Connecticut, arrived home from work on the evening of March 4, 1994, and found that his wife, Mabel, had stabbed herself fourteen times in the abdomen but, amazingly, had not succeeded in killing herself. Mabel begged him for more than an hour to bring her his gun. Convinced that Mabel was probably dying of her wounds anyway, Marland handed her a loaded .22-caliber pistol. When Mabel tried to fire the gun, it jammed. He reloaded the gun, gave it back to her, and watched as she shot herself. He waited a few hours before calling the police.

The medical examiner later reported that Mabel probably would have survived the stab wounds, but definitely not those from the gunshots. Marland was convicted of second-degree manslaughter even though, technically, Mabel's massacre was totally self-inflicted.

A twenty-three-year-old Egyptian woman named Rasha Mohamed Rajab called an ambulance, telling the dispatcher that
two thieves had broken into her home, killed her husband, and
attacked her with a knife. As it turned out, she was insanely
jealous. Literally.

Rasha said that her husband, Osama Musad, liked to look
at women. She imagined that he was having affairs with all of
them. So one night in 2008, while he slept, she electrocuted
him with a bare wire, then stabbed him a few times just to be
sure he was dead. She then put handfuls of money in her purse
and threw the bag out the window. She stabbed herself twice to
make the entire setup seem less suspicious.

When forced to come clean with the real story, Rasha told
the police she was insane at the time.

Irish pub owner Tom Nevin was described as a gentle giant who
was always eager to welcome strangers to his establishment with
open arms. His wife, Catherine, had a different opinion of him.
She saw herself as a woman stuck in a failed marriage. It would
appear the failure was mostly hers. She was reputed to sneak
strange men into her bedroom at the Galway pub known as Jack

White's Inn while her husband was busy working the bar. She could have walked away at any time, but she didn't want to leave empty-handed. So she hired a professional hit man to do away with Tom.

While Tom cashed out the register after a busy St. Patrick's Day weekend in 1996, Catherine's hit man pumped six bullets into him. He then tied Catherine up and stuffed a pair of panties into her mouth, as she had requested, to make the murder look like a botched robbery. Neither she nor the assassin thought to break a doorjamb or window to complete the charade. Police arrested Catherine when they realized there was no sign of forced entry.

Patricia Aldridge and her old flame, Mitchell Vickers, were one of those lucky couples who find each other again after many years of separation, and happily discover that their love is as true-blue and ooey-gooey as it ever was. Despite the obstacles and divergent paths their lives had taken, there was nothing beyond the remedy of true love, not even an extra spouse.

On June 26, 1998, Mitchell took a hammer and bludgeoned Patricia's husband, Millard Aldridge, to death, and torched his automobile. Mitchell surrendered to the police the day after

Millard's body was found and confessed to the crime. Patricia bailed him out of jail. They were both charged and convicted of murder, thus ensuring that they would spend the rest of their lives in separate prisons.

🦎

Relationships between mothers and daughters are notoriously difficult. An overprotective, secretive mother and a rebellious daughter can be a particularly deadly combination.

Brenda Linville of Uneeda, West Virginia, never disclosed the true identity of her sixteen-year-old daughter Morgan's father. Brenda was, by all accounts, a hardworking and kind woman who was utterly devoted to Morgan, though she took the girl out of traditional schools and educated her at home. She never allowed Morgan to go out on dates unsupervised.

In the winter of 2001, Morgan met a young man on the Internet, a nineteen-year-old named Paul Greenlief who was also being homeschooled and whose own mother described him as "kind of a loner." Within a month or two of knowing each other, Morgan began pressuring Paul to run away and get married.

To ensure Brenda Linville would not interfere, the young lovebirds bludgeoned the woman to death with a wooden plank. Then Morgan and Paul drove three miles from the house with

Brenda wrapped in a sheet. They put her behind the wheel of a purple Camaro and pushed the car into a ravine.

The plan to make it look like a car accident was so poorly staged and executed that the police immediately suspected foul play. There was nothing in the wreckage that matched the blows to Brenda's head. Witnesses saw Morgan and Paul speed away in the car Paul used to deliver pizzas. And when troopers arrived at the address under which the Camaro was registered, they found the driveway and porch covered in hair and blood.

Both Morgan and Paul are now serving life sentences, in separate prisons, of course.

Barbara Milburn of Millburn, West Virginia, said she was doing Judy Jenkins, her former lover, a favor by shooting her in the head. Barbara said Judy was despondent over a failed relationship with a man. Barbara could not, however, explain why she had also set fire to the barn next to the house they shared.

Ben Murray was a popular student at Memorial Middle School in Beverly, Massachusetts. His grades were mediocre, but he was a great lacrosse player. His mom, Gail Murray, was a well-loved English teacher at the same school.

Unsure whether he wanted to go to college after high school graduation, Ben worked a few odd jobs when he wasn't wandering around aimlessly. His last job was as a temporary postal worker during the holiday rush in December 1997.

On Christmas Eve, Ben and his mom got into an argument, and things got a little out of hand. He stabbed her in the chest twenty times with a paring knife, slit her throat, and bashed in her skull with a claw hammer. He then called 911 and calmly said to the operator, "Hi, I'd like to report a murder. I just killed my mother." When the operator pressed for more information, Ben said, "I thought I was doing the right thing, man."

At his arraignment, Ben pleaded innocent.

🐭

Edna Bursk of Blackpool, England, was the second wife of Brian Harris. She brought to the marriage a teenage daughter from a previous relationship. Brian had two daughters of his own, but as far as Edna and her sweet teen were concerned, there was no room in their new family for those children.

The newlyweds fought bitterly over the issue for twenty-one months. Finally, in 1985, Brian figured out how to make room for his beloved children. He grabbed a claw hammer and drove it three times into mean old Edna's head.

🐛

Beautiful Hajna, a twenty-five-year-old former fashion model and showgirl living in California, married a Hungarian physician eleven years her senior named Geza de Kaplany in 1962. A month later, in a jealous rage, Geza accused her of flirting with other men and of carrying on an affair. A terrible struggle ensued. Geza overpowered Hajna, bound and gagged her, mutilated her body with a knife, and injected a variety of acids into her wounds.

Neighbors called the police after hearing Hajna's screams, even over the thundering sounds of classical music blaring from the hi-fi at ear-splitting levels. Geza told the authorities that he had not killed his wife. It was one of his multiple personalities, he said, a guy named Pierre de la Roche.

🐛

A few days after Sarah Maria Louisa Kirwan was found dead on the rocky shores of a tiny uninhabited island and popular picnic spot called Ireland's Eye, her husband's mistress and their bastard children moved into the Kirwans' beautiful house in Dublin.

It was in September 1852 that her husband, William, took Sarah on a day trip to Ireland's Eye. William and Sarah had been quite happily married, but only for the first year or so. The rest of their years together deteriorated into a hopeless downward spiral of vitriolic bickering. At some point along the way, William took up with a young woman named Teresa Kenny from a town called Sandymount. Not long afterward, Teresa began referring to herself as Mrs. Kirwan, and then proceeded to give birth to William's children over the next few years.

On the day of their picnic, William asked the boatmen to pick him and Sarah up for the return trip at about 8 p.m. The last of the picnickers had left by 4, giving William plenty of time to wrap a wet sheet around Sarah's face and hold her underwater until she stopped thrashing. For a little while, people believed William's story that Sarah had actually drowned.

The truth came out during the inquest. The boatmen had reported seeing scratches on Sarah's body, and blood coming from her ears and mouth. Others who had been picnicking on Ireland's Eye that day came forward and reported having heard a lot of screaming and fighting. In a trial that lasted only four days, William was found guilty of murdering his wife and was sentenced to hang.

While awaiting his execution, William found Jesus in a big way. In the meantime, a number of prominent members of politics and society, whose prim Victorian principles dictated that such tasteless scandals and rude behavior be hidden behind closed doors, began circulating petitions and propaganda aimed at exonerating William. Despite the overwhelming evidence and flaws in the supporters' reasoning, William's death sentence was reduced to twenty-five years in prison and a one-way ticket to America, where he could live out the rest of his life and become somebody else's problem.

One hundred fifty years later, the case is still seen as one of the greatest miscarriages of justice in all of Ireland's legal history.

Seventy-six-year-old James Tomkinson shot his wife, Susan, many times in the head with a cordless nail gun. He then turned the tool on himself and fired several nails into his own head and chest. Family members found both of them dead in their Ocean Acres, New Jersey, home in August 2007.

Police were baffled by two things: First, why would a man kill his wife of fifty-five years with a nail gun, as opposed to something more effective and decisive, like a chainsaw? And second, why would he then commit suicide in exactly the same painful and torturous way? In an effort to shed some light on the glaringly obvious, the owner of a nearby tool rental center said of the makeshift weapon, "[The nails] don't really go that deep," which served only to explain why it took so many shots.

❧

Gareth MacDonald, a thirty-year-old pub manager from Wales, left his wife and three children when he fell in love with a former flight attendant named Glenn Rycroft. Then things got a little messy.

Years earlier, Glenn had swindled nearly a quarter of a million pounds from his family and friends. He quit his job with British Airways, claiming he had cancer, and shaved his head bald to be more convincing. He talked his brother into borrowing £10,000 and organized fund-raisers and raffles to raise money for an operation he said he needed in Australia. His "cure" consisted mostly of traveling all over the world like a king.

Gareth met Glenn on the Internet, and shortly afterward Gareth told his wife he was gay. The two men moved in together in February 2007. A few months later, Gareth noticed that his bank account was empty. He began to suspect that coming out as gay and hooking up with Glenn had probably been a mistake.

He sent a text message to his lover saying he was having trouble trusting him but that he still loved him.

Glenn and Gareth were staying at a Travelodge in Chester when their relationship ended for good in September 2007. Gareth confronted Glenn for the last time, and Glenn hit him over the head with a fire extinguisher. Twice.

Glenn tried to convince the police that it was all a tragic accident, that his fingerprints were all over the fire extinguisher because he and Gareth had been using the device to have sex.

8

HE NEEDED KILLIN'

The late southern humorist Lewis Grizzard often quipped that "he needed killin'" was a valid legal defense in Georgia.

All kidding aside, the pacifist in me was horrified to find that, under certain circumstances, I might actually agree with that.

If, for example, while in the course of causing grievous harm to some poor defenseless person, a vicious attacker were to, say, accidentally fall down an elevator shaft to a horrific and bloody death, my first reaction would likely be, "Well, at least *that* noise is over."

I know that's not nice, and certainly not very charitable, but I do so like the occasional shred of evidence that we do indeed live in a just universe.

For the most part, I trust that our justice system can pick up most of the slack when the universe doesn't come through. But I marvel at how neatly life—and death—can sometimes take care of its own.

Some of these stories seem ripped right out of the pages of the Manual of Divine Intervention. Others, thank goodness, are just plain dumb luck, hard at work for the good of all mankind.

Carl Hulsey, a seventy-seven-year-old retiree from Canton, Georgia, decided his white billy goat, Snowball, would make an excellent guard dog. Hulsey devised a training regimen that consisted mostly of his beating the poor animal with a stick to "make him mean." The plan worked.

On May 16, 1991, when Snowball saw Hulsey coming at him with his training stick, the little goat butted the old man in the stomach—twice. Hulsey ran up the porch steps with Snowball in hot pursuit. Hulsey's wife, Alma, watched as Snowball rammed the old man one last time, hurtling him five feet over the porch rail. Hulsey was pronounced dead right where he landed.

James Bahan was visiting his friend Christopher Frost in Conway, New Hampshire, when the two young men got into an argument. Christopher shot James with a twelve-gauge shotgun, hitting him in the right arm and chest. Amazingly, James lived.

While recuperating at his parents' house in West Paris, Maine, James got into an argument over the new living arrangements with his father, fifty-six-year-old Kevin Behan. At some point during the heated argument, James pulled out a deer-skinning knife with an eight-inch blade and stabbed his father. Horrified over what he had done, he turned the knife on himself. James's mother called the police, who arrived to find the father dead on the living room floor. James was mortally wounded but died before the LifeFlight helicopter made it to the scene.

While sitting in his prison cell awaiting trial on charges that he had killed his own son, fifty-two-year-old Dafydd Field from Surrey, England, had one last bright idea. He stuck his finger into a plug outlet and electrocuted himself. In a statement issued on April 10, 2007, a prison spokesman assured everyone that staff and paramedics had tried to resuscitate the man who had turned himself in to police when his son's body was found, but they were unsuccessful in their attempts to revive him. No one seemed particularly sorry to hear that.

※

Olof Palme, the prime minister of Sweden, was shot and killed in Stockholm in 1986 as he walked home from the movies with his wife. Christer Pettersson was tried and convicted of the murder. He was later acquitted and released from prison because the weapon was never found. Pettersson spent the rest of his life boasting about how he had gotten away with murder. The prime minister's assassination remains one of Sweden's great unsolved crimes.

In September 2004, Pettersson was admitted to Karolinska Hospital, unconscious and with severe head injuries. He died two weeks later of multiple organ failure and hemorrhaging of the brain. The cause of his injuries and subsequent death is also one of Sweden's most famous unsolved crimes. The difference is that, this time, far fewer Swedes were terribly shaken up by the news.

Richard Cooey and his buddy Clinton Dickens dropped a chunk of concrete from a highway overpass in Ohio on September 1, 1986, right onto a car driven by a college student named Wendy Offredo, whose passenger was her sorority sister Dawn McCreery. Richard and Clinton scrambled down the embankment, purportedly to help the two young women out of the wreckage. Instead they raped, robbed, beat, strangled, and mutilated the two young women, then threw their bodies into the woods.

After twenty-two years behind bars, Cooey was finally scheduled to die by lethal injection. His final appeal was based on the fact that prison food and confinement in a tiny jail cell had made him so obese that execution by lethal injection would not only be impossible, but it would cause him undue pain and suffering. He claimed there was no way the executioners would ever find a vein under all the flab on his five-foot-seven-inch, 267-pound body.

"There were no such difficulties," said Larry Greene of the Southern Ohio Correctional Facility. "He was vulgar and hateful to the end," said Summit County prosecutor Sherri Bevan Walsh.

Caryl Chessman, also known as the Red Light Bandit, made a living and passed the time by attacking, raping, and robbing people parked in secluded areas in and around Los Angeles. Lovers' lanes were his favorite spots.

Chessman was arrested in 1948 and admitted he had committed these crimes, but later said that police had "tortured" the confessions out of him. He was nonetheless sentenced to death.

He was scheduled to die in the gas chamber on May 2, 1960. A number of prominent people voiced their opposition to this execution, including such luminaries as Eleanor Roosevelt, Billy Graham, Norman Mailer, Robert Frost, and even the queen of Belgium. Federal Judge Louis Goodman was ultimately moved by these arguments and issued a stay of execution at the proverbial eleventh hour. His secretary, however, dialed the wrong number. When she finally did dial the correct number for the prison, she was informed that the cyanide pellets had already been dropped in the chamber. Chessman was forced to keep his date with the executioner.

During World War II, Dr. Marcel Petiot claimed to be a member of the Underground in France. He promised safe passage from

Paris to Argentina to a number of his Jewish patients. Instead he killed them and stole their money. He disposed of the corpses in a lime pit in his house and a homemade crematorium. After the liberation of France, authorities found twenty-seven decomposing corpses in Dr. Petiot's house. He was convicted of twenty-six of the murders but was suspected of killing more than sixty people in all. Dr. Petiot had his head whacked off in the guillotine in 1946.

Walter Wilkins was a doctor and landlord in New York City. In 1919, a beautiful young woman and her mother moved into one of the apartments in his home, and he soon fell madly in love with the daughter. He was not the first to succumb to the enchantment of the young woman's loveliness at first sight. Her name was Audrey Munson, and she was the inspiration and model for many of the most beautiful statues of female figures erected in New York and that still stand all across the city. One of the most famous of these is *Civic Fame*, the golden woman posing gracefully atop a large orb that rests on the cupola of City Hall.

Mrs. Wilkins was none too pleased with her husband's embarrassing displays of adolescent lust. She asked Munson and her mother to vacate the premises.

Right around that time, Dr. Wilkins called the police to their home to report that someone had burglarized his home and beaten his wife. Police found Julia Wilkins dead, and Dr. Wilkins's fingerprints all over a variety of murder weapons.

Dr. Wilkins was sentenced to death in the electric chair, but he hanged himself in his prison cell before the date of his execution.

Dr. Buck Ruxton was born Bukhtyar Rustomji Ratanji Hakim in Bombay, India. In 1927 he moved to Edinburgh, Scotland, where he met Isabella Van Ess. They moved to Lancashire in 1930 and hired a twenty-year-old nanny named Mary Rogerson to help care for their three children.

The couple's relationship was stormy at best. They often fought to the point of violence. Then around September 15, 1935, the Ruxton home became very quiet. Neighbors reported that Dr. Ruxton had started acting strangely. The maid told police that Dr. Ruxton had asked her to hose down the blood-spattered bathroom and burn a pile of bloodied clothes. Two weeks later, a human leg was found in the river Annan, carefully wrapped in newspaper. The date on the newspaper was September 15. Police found more body parts and incriminating evidence in their search of the Ruxton property.

Dr. Ruxton had killed his wife in a fit of rage. When he discovered that Mary the Nanny had witnessed the entire scene, he killed her, too.

Ruxton was found guilty of both murders in March 1936. Two months later, he was hanged at a prison called Strangeways.

Bruno Lüdke was one of Germany's worst serial killers. In a murdering frenzy that began in 1928 and lasted fifteen years, he is said to have butchered and sexually assaulted more than eighty-five people, most of them women. Although Germany had a certain knack for growing some of the world's most prolific killers during the early twentieth century (perhaps due to difficult economic times and an unstable political backdrop), what made Lüdke extra special was that he managed to elude detection despite the crushing hypervigilance of the Nazi regime.

However, Lüdke was finally caught, and the courts declared him insane. They sent him to a psychiatric facility in Vienna, Austria, for "treatment." Nazi doctors were happy to have him.

They performed countless experiments on the sadistic killer, purportedly in the name of justice and medical science. When they were done, they informed the courts that Lüdke had paid for his crimes by lethal injection.

🐒

Anatoly "The Terminator" Onoprienko freely admitted to killing fifty-two people with a sawed-off shotgun, an ax, and some knives in his native Ukraine. He killed the first nine in a violent robbery spree in 1989. He killed the other forty-three over a period of only six months. The fearsome animal was finally caught in April 1996. He stood inside an iron cage mostly staring at his own feet throughout his trial, looking very unlike a Terminator. The thirty-nine-year-old Onoprienko was bald, short, and thin, and was practically lost inside the enormous jacket he wore to court every day.

It took the judge two days to recite the entire verdict. Onoprienko was sentenced to die in the traditional Ukrainian way: a single gunshot to the back of the head. Onoprienko received the news with impassive calm. "I am not afraid of death," he said. "I've been close to death so many times that it's even interesting for me now to venture into the afterworld, to see what is there, after this death."

Joseph Colombo Sr., whose father was gunned down in a gangland war in the 1930s and whose sons later took over the family business, was one of the heads of New York's infamous Five Families in the 1960s. Colombo's business portfolio included such interests as gambling, hijacking, selling stolen merchandise, loan-sharking, and even a couple dozen or so legitimate commercial enterprises. The FBI was onto him, though, and Colombo took great offense over the harassment of himself and his family. He began to organize public protests to fight against the stereotyping of Italian-Americans.

During one such rally in midtown Manhattan's Columbus Circle in the summer of 1971, a young black man purportedly working for Joe Gallo, the head of one of the other Five Families, shot Colombo in front of hundreds of witnesses. The would-be assassin was immediately shot and killed right where he stood.

Colombo was nothing if not stubborn. It took him seven years to die of that gunshot wound.

Convicted murderer Michael Anderson Godwin had been scheduled to die in the electric chair in South Carolina's Central Correctional Institution, but his sentence was later commuted to life in prison. He was sitting naked on his stainless steel toilet one night in 1998, trying to fix a pair of headphones connected to his television set. He bit into the wires and electrocuted himself.

In 2007, almost eight years to the day, Laurance Baker met his maker in much the same way. Baker was another murderer serving a life sentence. Guards at the Allegheny County Prison in Pittsburgh, Pennsylvania, found Baker dead in his cell, sitting on his aluminum toilet, pants puddled around his ankles, and wearing a set of homemade headphones. He, too, had accidentally electrocuted himself.

Charles Martin loved his lawn. The sixty-seven-year-old man from Batavia, Ohio, fussed over every blade, cut it every five days, watered it, and tended to it like a lover. Larry Mugrage Jr., a local high school boy, knew exactly how important Martin's lawn was to him. So Mugrage stepped on the lawn every chance he got, just to watch Martin lose his mind.

In March 2006, as Mugrage was walking to a friend's house, he decided to take a stroll through Martin's lawn. Martin shot out of his house and started screaming at the boy, who was delighted to exchange a few words and gestures with the old man. At the end of their encounter, Mugrage went on his merry way, and Martin went inside the house and loaded his .410-gauge shotgun. He sat on his porch with the shotgun in his lap and waited. He waited for more than three hours. As far as Martin was concerned, Mugrage's comeuppance was long overdue. The kid had it coming.

When Mugrage headed back from his friend's house, he made a little detour, right across Martin's lawn. The old man shot the kid twice. He then went inside and dialed 911. "I just killed a kid," he told the dispatcher.

Martin will be eligible for parole in 2025.

Alejandra Galeana, a thirty-year-old pharmacy clerk from Mexico City, went missing in October 2007. On a tip, police went to the apartment of a young man she had recently started dating. When they got there, the boyfriend was in the middle of dinner, but he ran out into the street and was hit by a car. He survived and was taken to the hospital while police took a look around the apartment.

They found Alejandra's torso in Jose Luis Calva's closet. One of her legs was in the refrigerator, and some of her bones were in a cereal box. The meat that was in the frying pan, as well as the half-eaten food on Jose's plate—all belonged to Alejandra.

Jose told police he was a writer and a poet. Investigators found the draft of a novel titled *Cannibalistic Instincts*.

Jose was awaiting trial on murder charges, suspected of killing and dismembering at least three other women. To the prosecutors' chagrin, Jose hanged himself in his jail cell before they could get him to trial.

❧

When seventy-four-year-old murderer Aladena "Jimmy the Weasel" Fratianno learned that he would no longer be sheltered by the Witness Protection Program, his first reaction was, "I'm a dead man!"

Inducted into the program in 1981, Fratianno had helped the Justice Department convict at least thirty murderers, including six Mafia bosses. In return for his services, he received a stipend of $730 a month, and additional federal "support" totaling about $1 million. Prosecutors also agreed to go easy on him after he confessed to his own involvement in eleven other killings. He served only twenty-one months of a five-year sentence.

As Fratianno became one of the longest-surviving inductees of the program, it was, perhaps, inevitable that the U.S. Marshals Service began to worry that other criminals would start thinking that Witness Protection was a sort of retirement fund for ex-thugs.

So the feds turned Fratianno loose in 1992. A spokesman for the department told reporters, "He can make it on his own."

Despite his many fears and loud protests, Fratianno did, in fact, do a fine job making it on his own without getting whacked. There certainly are people in the world who think all snitches deserve to die, but none of them ever came looking for Fratianno in the years following his return to the world of regular folk. Nevertheless, rumors did persist (mostly from Fratianno) that there was a contract on his life.

Fratianno made several appearances as a celebrity hoodlum on television programs such as *60 Minutes,* and was immortalized in a few film documentaries on Mafia crime families. Book royalties from the publication of two autobiographies also helped keep him solvent.

Fratianno died in his sleep in 1993 at the age of seventy-nine. The exact location of his death and burial remains a secret.

❧

When Andrei Chikatilo was a little boy growing up in the inhospitable frozen wastelands of rural Ukraine in the 1930s, his parents often told him stories about his older brother. "We were very poor and very hungry. So when he died, we ate him."

Andrei heard many stories like this growing up, from other relatives and neighbors. Starvation and want were then so commonplace in that part of the world that cannibalism had become the least of their moral shortcomings. But while other Ukrainians learned to live in relative harmony with this macabre reality, this knowledge planted the initial seeds of the man Andrei would become.

In a massive manhunt spanning twelve years and several Russian jurisdictions, the monster who would come to be known as the Rostov Ripper was finally caught in 1992. He was convicted of brutally butchering fifty-three people, many of whom he snacked on. On February 16, 1994, he was executed in the customary Ukrainian way—with a single bullet to the back of the head.

🐗

The torched and decapitated body of Daniel Gene-Vincent Sorensen of River Rouge, Michigan, was found by a construction crew in November 2007. The burns on his hands were particularly bad, as if in a deliberate effort to hide the man's identity. Police were able to use enough of the partial prints to confirm Sorensen's identity. He turned out to be a registered sex offender. Whoever killed him probably had a very good reason.

A thirty-two-year-old man named Arthur Ruiz and his mother, Guadalupe, rented a small room in a boardinghouse in La Habra, California. In the two months that they lived there, they had made the acquaintance of the other boarders, who thought Guadalupe was a nice and respectful person, but worried about the son. Arthur liked walking around slumped over, with his head buried in the hood of his jacket.

In May 2007, one of the boarders called 911 and reported some kind of disturbance in Arthur and Guadalupe's room. Police arrived to find Guadalupe lying in one of the beds with her head sawn off. Arthur was lying dead on the floor with a bloody circular saw near his hand. After killing his mother, he had chopped off his most of his own head with the same tool.

Paul Stephens began arguing with his twenty-one-year-old girlfriend, Lorena Godoy Osorio, in their Dallas apartment one Thursday evening in June 2004. No one knows for sure what they were arguing about, but all it did was get worse from there.

Neighbors say they saw Lorena getting into Paul's Mercedes coupe. The thirty-five-year-old man hurled a rock through the driver's side window, got into the car, and drove away with Lorena still inside.

The car stopped on the Bush overpass on Texas Road 190, about fifteen miles away. Passing drivers saw the two fighting, and at least one of them stopped to see if he could help the woman, who was clearly being overpowered by the man. Henry Ford of Plano, Texas, was one of these motorists. But before he could get out of his car, Paul had thrown Lorena over the side of the overpass. She landed on a car passing below on the North Central Expressway, fell off a short distance away, and was killed when the car she had landed on and then another car ran over her.

Paul beheld his handiwork in horror from the top of the overpass, and decided, perhaps a bit too late, to do the right thing: He threw himself over the edge of the overpass to his own death.

The botched execution of Florida inmate Allen Lee Davis in July 1999 was a story for the ages. The state had an electric chair specially made to accommodate the 350-pound convicted killer, but something went horribly wrong anyway.

Before he was pronounced dead, Davis seems to have exploded. He began bleeding from the mouth and through the chest. Blood puddled in the center of his white shirt and oozed through the buckle holes of the strap that was holding him upright in the chair.

When Florida Supreme Court Justice Leander Shaw saw color photographs of the executed man, he said, "For all appearances, [Davis] was brutally tortured to death by the citizens of Florida."

State Senator Ginny Brown-Waite was a witness to the execution. She said that at first she was shocked by the sight of all that blood. However, when she realized the stain had begun to form the shape of a cross, she took it as a sign that God himself approved of this execution.

Louis Mockewich was shoveling snow from the patio of his Philadelphia home during the winter of 2003. The problem was that he was piling it against the side of Michael Kilpatrick's pickup truck. When Michael complained, Louis shot him dead.

Louis was sentenced to thirty years in prison. Apparently, "He needed killin'" is not a valid defense in the City of Brotherly Love.

9

GAMBLING WITH THE RENT MONEY

Deep in my strange little twisted heart and in every crooked joint of my soul, I believe the world is made up mostly of decent people just trying to get from one day to the next without setting themselves on fire or accidentally cooking the cat.

And yet, such things happen.

Sometimes we take dumb risks. We forget that we're mortal and we're fragile, and that other people are, too. We miscalculate the odds or forget that we really suck at math. We behave as if life were a game of checkers when it's really a game of chess.

And still, at other times, no matter how hard we try or how carefully we move the pieces on the board, at some point or another we all come face-to-face with the ugly reality of that old adage "No one dies a virgin. Life screws us all." The worst part of it, though, is when we screw ourselves.

I don't think very many of the people in these stories ever set out to do real harm. But we should all be grateful that their extraordinary acts of stupidity were mostly accidental.

Ronald Long of Deepwater, Missouri, bought a new flat-screen TV in March 2008. He was pretty handy with tools and such, so he decided to mount it on the wall himself. However, he ran into some difficulties trying to punch a hole through the exterior wall of his house. Having exhausted his reserve of conventional tools and techniques, he decided to blow a couple of openings through the wall with a .22-caliber handgun. His wife, Patsy, was standing outside at the time, on the other side of the wall.

Interestingly, she did not run or scream after hearing the first shot. It was the second bullet that killed her.

In November 2007, train inspectors in Yekaterinburg, Russia, thought the object in passenger Mikhail Ershov's pocket looked suspiciously more like a hand grenade than a commuter rail ticket. They ordered Ershov off the train, at which point the probably inebriated man pulled the pin out of the grenade and demanded to be taken to Vladivostok, thousands of miles away.

Authorities immediately began negotiating with Ershov while the other train passengers were evacuated. They were finally able to talk him into putting the pin back into the grenade, but he missed. The grenade blew up, and so did Ershov. No one else was hurt.

Kindhearted Glenn Hollinshead, a forty-one-year-old man from Stoke-on-Trent, England, opened up his home to Sabina Eriksson from County Cork, Ireland, in May 2008 and offered her a place to stay for the night when he learned she had nowhere else to go. As thanks for his hospitality, Sabina stabbed him in the chest. She then hit herself on the head with a hammer and jumped off a nearby road bridge.

Sabina survived the ordeal. Good Samaritan Glenn did not.

Farida Begun, a Pakistani woman in her seventies who was visiting her family in the Elmhurst section of Queens in New York City, sat down to a quiet dinner with her daughter-in-law, Ayesha Akter, one Saturday night in the summer of 2003. Ayesha asked Farida to please pass the rice. Farida thought she would pass along a little sage wisdom to her chubby daughter-in-law instead.

Farida told Ayesha that rice was too fattening for her and refused the young woman's request. So Ayesha picked up a meat cleaver and gave Farida a few well-placed whacks. She hit the old woman in the head, chest, legs, arms, and hands, chopping off one of Farida's fingers in the process.

Farida died soon after the attack. Neighbors described both women as fat.

Lola Mae Barker of Madison, West Virginia, was described by her son as "a good Christian woman," but she was certainly no ordinary helpless old lady. She was an astute businesswoman and often had large amounts of cash in her purse.

In 1999, three people came to her home and made off with her purse. The seventy-three-year-old Lola Mae got into her car and went after the hoodlums. The chase led down an isolated country road. One of the robbers, Trisha Justice, fired three shots into Lola Mae's car. All three shots hit Lola Mae in the head, killing her instantly.

๛

Dion John Stabe, a thirty-one-year-old drug dealer from Brisbane, Australia, was distraught over having broken up with his girlfriend the morning of November 27, 1997. He was a regular user of the hallucinogenic LSD, and frequently snorted speed, but that day he decided to wash down some amphetamines with a bottle of liquid deodorant and some scented oil. He then made his way to a neighbor's house, ripped the hinges off the back door, and let himself in.

When the neighbor returned from a shopping trip with her five-year-old son, she found Dion dead on the floor of her kitchen, lying in a large pool of blood. He had stabbed himself repeatedly in the legs and chest with a steak knife, a can opener, and a nail file.

Dion's brother, Ray, said it was a clear case of murder. The coroner was pretty certain it was a suicide. The ex-girlfriend's explanation was that Dion was a bit paranoid and often saw ninjas watching him through the windows.

Sirkka Sari was a Finnish actress of strikingly intense good looks and all of nineteen years old when she was cast in the 1939 movie *A Rich Girl*. While attending a cast party at the Hotel Aulanko, Sirkka stepped out onto a balcony for a bit of fresh air.

The party took place on one of the higher floors of the hotel. Sirkka was known to be adventurous and utterly unafraid of heights. For reasons known only to her, she decided to climb to the top of a chimney, where she lost her footing and fell right in. She landed on a boiler, which killed her instantly.

Arthur Warren Waite was a dentist who, for fun, liked growing bacteria in his home laboratory and poring over books on toxicology. He met and married the daughter of wealthy drug manufacturer John Peck. As a gift, the Pecks bought the newlyweds a posh home on New York City's Riverside Drive.

In January 1916, while Hannah Peck was visiting her daughter and son-in-law, she became extremely ill. Arthur had secretly laced his mother-in-law's food with influenza and diphtheria. She died very quickly, and her body was shipped back to Michigan for cremation and burial.

Distraught over the death of his beloved wife, John Peck went to New York a couple months later to grieve with his daughter and son-in-law. Arthur decided to repeat his earlier experiment, which had worked so beautifully.

John Peck turned out to be impervious to diphtheria. He continued to grieve and eat tainted food, much to Arthur's consternation.

Arthur decided to try another approach. He talked John into trying out a new nasal spray. Arthur had infused the liquid with colonies of tuberculosis germs. John never even cleared his throat.

Arthur then started lacing John's food with calomel, or mercurous chloride, which is most often used in laxatives and insecticides. Arthur hoped that a high enough dose of the colorless, tasteless compound would either kill John with a spectacular case of explosive diarrhea or sufficiently weaken his immune system so that the tuberculosis or diphtheria could finally kick in. It was as if the old man's innards were lined with lead.

Arthur finally decided to up the ante with a good old-fashioned dose of arsenic. That did the trick.

John Peck's son became suspicious enough of his parents' untimely deaths that he convinced the authorities to perform an autopsy on his father. Sure enough, the medical examiner found sufficient evidence to charge Arthur with murder. Had he been a little more patient and not placed the easy bet on arsenic as the sure thing, Arthur might have gotten away with it. Instead, he fried in Sing Sing's electric chair in 1917.

In March 1982, Ozzy Osbourne and his heavy metal band were on tour, traveling through Florida. Ozzy and several others were on the tour bus, and the band's lead guitarist, Randy Rhoads, was traveling in a light plane with two other people. Randy and the pilot thought it would be great fun to "buzz" the tour bus. This quickly proved to be a terrible idea.

The plane's wing crashed into the back of the bus, shattering the vehicle to smithereens. The plane then spun out of control and crashed into a house. The plane burst into flames, killing everyone on board. The house burned to the ground, but none of the occupants were harmed. Ozzy did not understand what had happened until someone explained it to him later.

A fifty-year-old woman from Brisbane, Australia, was on vacation with her husband in the central western Queensland town of Longreach. They were having dinner at the Happy Valley Chinese Restaurant on October 25, 2007, when the missus asked to be seated at a different table because the air-conditioning vent was blowing cold air directly on her. The waitstaff was happy to oblige.

An unidentified young woman from Longreach pulled into the parking lot of the Happy Valley Chinese Restaurant that lovely October day. Once out of the car, she noticed that she hadn't parked quite as close to the curb as she should have, so she got back in and tried again. She eased the car into the space, but then kept going. She drove through the glass front and into the restaurant, running over a couple of middle-age tourists from Brisbane.

The woman who had complained about the air-conditioning was the only fatality.

Ariel Figueroa, a twenty-four-year-old man from Hackensack, New Jersey, loved his BMW 325 and fancied himself an excellent driver. In February 2002, several people called the police to report a man driving erratically along Route 80 in Roxbury. He would sometimes slow the car to about ten or twenty miles per hour, and then suddenly accelerate to speeds exceeding one hundred. Most of the time, he was driving with his head and shoulders sticking outside the driver's side window, and other times while standing up through the sunroof. All the while, he was swerving around other cars and making crazy lane changes.

Ariel's wild ride finally ended when his Beamer swerved into a grassy embankment, hit a tree stump, became airborne, and finally hit a utility pole about thirty feet above the ground. Police arrived to find him pinned underneath what was left of his car, which was crumpled at the base of the pole. He was halfway out of the sunroof. He was pronounced dead at the scene.

~

Olivia Goldsmith once had great aspirations of becoming a high-powered CEO. To get herself started on that path, she established her own business, teaching secretaries how to use computers. Soon she discovered that the corporate world bored her to tears. So she came up with another dream: She would become a great British author. Even though she was from New Jersey.

Amazingly, Olivia actually made her second dream come true. In the early 1990s, she sold the rights to her debut novel, *The First Wives' Club,* to a London publisher for the unprecedented amount of £2 million sterling.

Olivia was a master at reinventing herself, inside and out. In addition to her various professional incarnations, she had three different names (her birth name, Randy Goldsmith, and later Justine Rendal), lied about her age, and was obsessed with cosmetic surgery.

It was this last obsession that proved to be her undoing. While under anesthesia to remove the sagging skin from her chin (which became droopy as a result of the numerous procedures she had undergone to suck the fat out of her throat), she suffered a heart attack and never regained consciousness. She was removed from life support in January 2004, at the presumed age of fifty-four.

A year before she died, Olivia wrote an article for a magazine called *Night & Day*. In it, she said she wanted her funeral to take place in Westminster Abbey, an open-casket affair in which she would be laid out in a bikini—after the undertaker performed a whole lot more liposuction on her corpse. Alas, she died at Lenox Hill Hospital in New York and was buried at an undisclosed location.

In December 2009, a twenty-five-year-old Ukrainian chemistry student named Vladimir Likhonos developed a nasty habit of dipping his chewing gum in powdered citric acid to prolong the taste. While he was studying in his room one night, his family heard a very loud popping sound. When they went to investigate, they found Vladimir with half of his face missing. The aspiring scientist had apparently dipped his gum into the wrong compound and inadvertently created a small bomb. Unfortunately, it was big enough to make his head explode.

Armadillos may be a little smarter than most people think, maybe even smarter than some zookeepers.

On a chilly night in November 2007, an armadillo at the Indianapolis Zoo moved its bedding a little closer to an overhead heating lamp that was double-chained to the ceiling and hung about two feet off the floor of the Critter Corner exhibit. Unfortunately, the material used for the animals' bedding was highly flammable. When the smoke cleared, the armadillo, three turtles, two birds, a snake, and several other small animals made the place look more like the Crispy Critters Corner. They were all dead.

John Dominic Robertson died doing it doggie-style … sort of. A great aficionado of kinky sex games, and unable or unwilling to convince his wife to play along, the fifty-six-year-old man made friends with the younger and more adventurous Margaret Bradley. While visiting Margaret in December 2001, things got a little out of hand.

Police found John chained to a wall. He was wearing only socks and a dog collar. In this position and thusly attired, and having previously snorted an amyl-nitrate popper, he asphyxiated while having sex with Margaret. The collar wasn't fastened too tightly, but the slightly built woman wasn't strong enough to lift him off the wall when he slumped over. She had to call for help. John's wife, coincidentally also named Margaret, was brought in to identify the body.

Four grown men from Fairfax County, Virginia, laid down on the tracks near a commuter rail station for a predawn game of "chicken" in the summer of 1994. Chad Rochette, David Blalock, Don Hunsinger, and Dave Skelly were crushed, splattered, and strewn under the weight of the 144-car, 6,000-ton Norfolk Southern train. The men, ranging in age from eighteen to twenty-one, apparently believed that if they arranged themselves lengthwise between the tracks instead of perpendicularly across them, the train would easily roll over them without touching them. They were wrong. Police found and tried to reassemble the hundreds of body parts scattered across a 250-foot stretch of the tracks.

꩜

Truly serious holiday shoppers don't let anything get in the way of cashing in on the Black Friday sales—not even live human beings.

On the day after Thanksgiving in 2008, a suburban New York Wal-Mart store was scheduled to open at sunrise. Early birds were promised unbelievable bargains in the first couple hours of the store's operations. Approximately two thousand people stood outside the store's main entrance and braved the cold weather for a chance at picking up cheap toys and electronics.

When the doors were finally unlocked, customers broke from the otherwise orderly line in which they had stood all night and, in some cases, since early Thanksgiving morning. The crowd turned into a massive uncaged animal. They ripped the doors from their hinges and literally exploded through glass doors and windows. A few people were hurt, including a slow-moving pregnant woman. Another woman struggled under the weight of people literally walking on her back as a way of stepping over some kind of obstacle blocking the entrance.

The obstacle turned out to be Jdimytai Damour, a 270-pound, thirty-four-year-old temporary worker hired by Wal-Mart to help with crowd control. Despite his great size and youthful strength, he was trampled to death almost immediately. Other store security employees tried to slow the rush of customers and empty the store, but people just kept shopping and fighting with one another over the merchandise, in the traditional way.

The Occupational Safety and Health Administration (OSHA) issued Wal-Mart a "serious citation" for failing to keep its employees safe and asked the multibillion-dollar enterprise to pay a fine of $7,000.

~

As far as anyone could tell, Stella Chambers of Michigan City, Indiana, was not in financial difficulty of any kind. She simply enjoyed living frugally. On the night of January 23, 2008, at the age of sixty-one, she froze to death in her own bed.

When the police entered Stella's home, they found the windows iced over and the water in the toilet bowl frozen solid. When they pulled back the covers of her bed, they found that Stella was wearing a hat.

The grand old American tradition of playing "chicken"—running across the railroad tracks before the oncoming train runs you over—got a new twist in the 1980s. The game was called "tracking" instead of "chicken," and it was played in the dark tunnels of New York City's subways, not in the wide open spaces of the railway system. And, as if "chicken" wasn't a stupid enough invention, "tracking" involved running the *length* of the train tracks between stations, not the four and a half feet or so *across* the tracks. So, of course, idiots died.

Jean Guerrier, a junior high school student from Brooklyn, was "tracking" with several other friends in the Union Street station. When the crew heard the roar of an oncoming train, most of them guessed correctly that it was time to step over to the express track, which ran parallel to the one they were on. Young Jean froze. He was promptly pureed by the oncoming train.

One of the surviving "tracking" geniuses told a friend that Jean was probably surprised by the train that hit him.

When police arrived at the third floor of Stradley Hall at Ohio State University on October 27, 2006, they found half of Andy

Polakowski sprawled out facedown in the hallway. The other half of him was dangling into the elevator that had gotten stuck between floors.

The elevator was full of students standing shoulder to shoulder, all twenty-four of them on their way out for a night of merriment. "Polo," as he was called, was the last person to squeeze inside the eighty-by-fifty-inch car.

The elevator began its descent before the doors were completely closed, very possibly because the weight of the students was more than 1,000 pounds over the 2,500-pound limit. The car suddenly stopped midway down from the third floor landing. Polo, who was a slightly built young man, decided to hop off before the elevator started moving again. He wasn't quick enough. As he was half in and half out of the elevator, it began to descend. The doors closed around his waist and the roof crushed his midsection against the floor of the hallway.

When rescuers arrived, they shone a flashlight into the small gap above Polo and between the doors, and onto the pale, silent faces of the twenty-three other students still inside.

꙳

David Daloia and James O'Hare, a couple of down-on-their-luck buddies in their sixties, shared an apartment with an even more hapless pal, Virgilio Cintron. In better days, Cintron had been a garden-variety street hustler with a long rap sheet. He and O'Hare had been friends for four decades. As Cintron's health deteriorated in recent years, Daloia had joined them to help with Cintron's care and ease the burden of maintaining a New York City apartment, even one in Hell's Kitchen.

On the evening of January 9, 2008, Daloia and O'Hare propped Cintron in an old office chair and wheeled him down Ninth Avenue to the Pay-O-Matic check-cashing place. Witnesses reported that the man in the chair kept flopping from side to side while the others kept trying to keep him from falling off the chair. Daloia and O'Hare parked Cintron outside the Pay-O-Matic and went in to cash Cintron's $355 Social Security check.

The clerk wouldn't cash the check without inspecting Cintron, and the two would-be customers argued that their friend was indisposed at the moment. Meanwhile, a crowd had gathered to gawk at the dead guy in the chair. Police arrested Daloia and O'Hare.

The case against the two still-living friends was dismissed because they claimed that Cintron had been alive when they left the apartment, and the coroner could not prove that he had not died outside the check-cashing place, as Daloia and O'Hare claimed.

Unlucky Stiffs

The caper made international headlines. Daloia couldn't believe he and his buddies had achieved such notoriety. Outside the courthouse, Daloia told reporters, "I thought Britney Spears took her pants down again."

Juan Flores Lopez of San Angelo, Texas, was distraught over the news that his wife wanted a divorce and that she didn't want him in the house anymore. For months, the forty-seven-year-old man kept threatening to set fire to himself and the house.

On June 19, 2007, officers were called to the family's residence, where they found Juan holding a gas can in one hand and a cigarette lighter in the other. When the police tried to subdue him, Juan tried tossing gasoline at them. There was no talking Juan down from his rant, so the cops Tasered him. Juan, who had already doused himself with the gas, immediately burst into flames. He died a short time later.

Randle Cunningham, a twenty-two-year-old man from Colorado Springs, Colorado, was driving around town with a stolen .380-caliber semiautomatic handgun tucked into his waistband.

He stopped at a Taco Bell drive-through window at about 1:45 a.m. on Halloween night 2005.

He paid the server for the food order, but dropped some of the change. When he opened the car door and leaned over to pick up the coins that had fallen to the ground, the gun discharged, shooting him in the groin. The server at the window said Randle said something unintelligible, put the gun on the passenger seat, and let the car drift a few feet away. When police arrived a few minutes later, Randle was dead.

🐌

In 1998, a doomsayer named José Ricart from Burgos, Spain, was walking up and down the street carrying a sign that said, "The End of the World Is Nigh." And so it was, at least for him. A truck ran over him and killed him.

10

WHISKEY TANGO FOXTROT*

Anytime you start to get comfortable with the notion that you've pretty much seen and heard it all, think about this: At any given moment in time, there are millions of people in the world—and at least as many animals—doing things to themselves or to each other that you haven't even begun to imagine.

Just think about that for a second.

It's happening. Right now.

---

* WTF, or "What the fuck...?"

And if that doesn't make you want to run away screaming or hide under the bed, then you may be one of those people the rest of us are trying not to imagine.

Some of the things we do as humans—and therefore, some of the ways in which we do ourselves in—defy all comprehension. How can someone die by simply sitting on a sofa? By sitting there for six or seven years. Impossible, you say? Read on.

Florida resident Gayle Grinds was a whole lot of woman—and then some. She was four feet, ten inches and weighed nearly five hundred pounds. Her husband, Herman Thomas, said he had tried for six years to coax her onto her feet, to no avail. Because she was unable to move, even to use the bathroom, the lower half of her body had literally fused to the sofa.

In August 2004, Grinds's brother called emergency medical technicians because his sister was having trouble breathing. The cause was probably the filth and unventilated stench in which Grinds had been living for years.

EMTs clad in haz-mat suits and breathing apparatuses embarked on a six-hour effort to rescue the woman. Unable to separate her from the furniture, it took twelve Martin County Fire-Rescue workers to move her—couch and all—onto a trailer hitched to a pickup truck. Grinds was taken to Martin Memorial Hospital South, where she died a short time later, still fused to the sofa.

♊

Rugby is undoubtedly one of the world's roughest sports. A popular bumper sticker proclaims, "Give Blood. Play Rugby." By extension, the game's players are built to endure real punishment.

Rugby champ Aled Evans from Liverpool, England, fell twenty-five feet through the roof of a shed in April 2008, and literally broke his head. Even so, he lived two more weeks before finally giving up the ghost.

♊

On January 15, 1997, Bakersfield, California, police arrived at the home of forty-four-year-old Avon Griffis to find her seventy-seven-year-old mother, Elizabeth Wilcher, sitting quietly and neatly dressed on the living room sofa. Authorities estimated that Wilcher had been dead for about five months. Her eyes were wide open.

Griffis explained to the police that her mother was suffering from "demonical depression" and that she would wake up any minute.

Less than a week later and about one hundred miles away, Fresno police encountered an almost identical scene. They found sixty-three-year-old Geraldine Bennett in a bedroom of the home she shared with her son, John. She had been dead at least a year. Her son was unable to understand that his mother was dead, and he was taken to a psychiatric facility for care.

No foul play was suspected in the deaths of either of the women, but it appears Griffis had continued to deposit her mother's Social Security checks as usual over the course of her mother's demonical depression.

❧

Joe and Christine Smith from West Boldon, England, were devastated when they found their beloved twelve-year-old Labrador, Brit, dead in the garden with his head stuck in a plastic chicken wrapper. They surmise that the wind must have blown the bag out of the trash receptacle on that fateful day in January 2008, and the aroma of cooked chicken was just too much for sweet Brit to resist. He stuck his whole head in the back to lick the juices at the bottom, and suffocated himself in the process. The

Smiths later embarked on a campaign to require all grocers to use perforated plastic bags for their cooked meat and poultry products, or wrap them in aluminum foil.

᠅

The Florida Everglades are a popular dumping ground for exotic pets such as boa constrictors, iguanas, and other critters that have outlived their cuteness. The alligators don't much appreciate their natural habitats being overrun by these illegal aliens, except of course when the intruders are small enough to eat.

In October 2005, a gator and an expatriated Burmese python got into something of a scuffle over which one would become that evening's dinner. The python, weighing more than one hundred pounds and measuring nearly thirteen feet in length, decided to eat a six-foot Florida alligator, headfirst. Not one to go down without a fight, the gator snapped its powerful jaws from *inside* the snake and tried to claw its way out through its midsection.

Both creatures were found dead at the scene—the python split through the middle with most of the alligator still inside it. The strangest thing of all, however, was that the python's head was missing.

It was not known whether the gator bit the python's head off on the way in, or if it reared back and clamped its teeth over the snake's head after it had chewed and clawed most of its way out of the snake. It is also possible that some other hungry creature passing by decided to snack on the leftovers.

Despite the fact that William "Rusty" Redfern of Tucker, Georgia, was born with no arms, he made quite a name for himself as an artist. His pen-and-ink drawings, which could take as long as six months apiece to complete because he had to do them with his foot, won him serious national acclaim in the 1980s. In recent years, he was living happily ever after with the former girlfriend of Charles Teer.

Charles and Rusty got into a fight over said girlfriend outside Charles's house in Snellville, Georgia, in September 2007. It was not the first time the two had fought over the woman. Words escalated into real fighting when Rusty kicked Charles and Charles hit him back. Bystanders stepped in to separate the two, but Rusty went back for one more shot. He stepped up to Charles and head-butted him. Charles took a step back and said, "I'm dizzy," then fell down dead in his own driveway.

Triple bypass surgery at the relatively young age of forty-seven may have forced John Blake to take it easy and quit his job, but it never stopped the cheerful guy from appreciating a beautiful sunny day or tending to his garden in the small town of Bromyard in Herefordshire, England.

Fifteen years after that life-changing surgery, on a lovely early autumn day in 2008, John and his wife decided to trim the twelve-foot hedges that surrounded their bungalow. John slipped on the stepladder and impaled himself through the torso on a tall metal spike attached to a fence post. It took five paramedics to de-skewer him, but by then, he was well on his way to the next life.

In August 2009, Cecilia Casals spritzed herself with some flammable liquid, set herself on fire, and took a stroll through a Miami shopping mall. Witnesses reported seeing the woman walking very slowly, silently, with her arms outstretched and completely covered in flames for two and a half minutes. Armed with fire extinguishers, two people doused her with foam and were able to put her out, but by then she had lost consciousness. A week later she was dead.

Christopher Bacon, a Welsh showroom worker at a car dealership, fell down some stairs and broke a few bones in his neck. He was able to get around for a while but had to wear a neck brace and often complained of excruciating pain. About a month after the accident and no longer able to take the pain, he left his house in the middle of the night and went into the woods, where he stabbed himself twenty times in the neck. A dog walker found his body the next day.

As Jamie Brown went about his daily work routine of sweeping the sidewalks in front of the Empire State Building in New York City one lovely spring afternoon in 2007, a human leg came crashing down from the sky, landing with a loud *boom* right in front of him. He stared at the object in disbelief, slowly realizing that, were it not for a few inches, there might have been two deaths that day.

Staff at the law offices of Levine & Blit on the sixty-ninth floor told police that a man in his thirties, not an employee of the firm, had slowly made his way to a window and begun to ease his way out of it before anyone realized what he was doing. The man, whom police would not identify, jumped to his death but hit a parapet halfway down, which severed his leg. While most of the jumper's body remained lodged in the parapet, his severed leg continued to fall to the street below. It landed directly in front of an eatery called Café Europa, which was filled with tourists who had stopped in for a quick bite. As the diners and passersby stopped to look—and realized what they were looking at—people began to faint in horror.

Meanwhile, business went on as usual inside the city landmark. Police conducted their investigation without having to inconvenience the long line of visitors waiting to go one hundred stories up to the observation deck.

Dennis Roache, a thirty-four-year-old man from St. Petersburg, Florida, did not take the news well that his ex-girlfriend had started dating another man. On February 4, 2002, Dennis broke into the home of his perceived rival, Gregory Shannon, and attacked him with a machete. Then he chopped his head off.

Dennis took Gregory's head outside and placed it on the hood of an Oldsmobile Cutlass Supreme. He then arranged a mirror in front of Greg's head so he could "see" himself. Shocked neighbors looked on.

Dennis was found competent to stand trial. It took the jury two hours to find him guilty of first-degree murder. He's currently serving a life sentence.

🐛

Ola Burnkert, best known as the drummer for the 1970s Swedish pop band ABBA, was found dead in his home in Spain in March 2008. He had fallen through the glass door leading out to the patio, and one of the shards had cut a major artery in his neck. He bled to death a few steps away, in the garden.

🐛

Rachel Greenway, a thirty-two-year-old interior designer from Staffordshire, England, was taking a peaceful stroll in her little garden one afternoon in the summer of 2000. She slipped on the steps and got a nasty bump on the head, but she was well enough to cry out for help. Neighbors heard her, and someone called the paramedics. When they got there, they found that Greenway had lost consciousness while waiting for help to arrive and fallen face-first into a small fishpond. She might have survived the bump on the head, but drowned in twelve inches of pond water.

A homeless man sleeping in a Dumpster outside a Miami furniture store was accidentally killed when the city garbage truck came by to empty the container in September 1997. The man's head was found inside the Dumpster. His body was found in a landfill two days later.

A man claiming to be the Angel Gabriel (his real name was Trevor Clancy) was denied entry to the SGI nightclub in Fermoy, Ireland, on New Year's Eve 2006. Security personnel at the club noticed that he was carrying an awfully big assortment of knives, so they called the Garda Síochána (Guardians of the Peace of Ireland) to assist. Garda Tracey Whelan and Sergeant John Liston called for backup when they were unable to persuade Trevor to hand over the knives. At least ten officers tried to disarm Trevor by beating him with their nightsticks and spraying him with a fire extinguisher, but Trevor continued to slash at them. When Trevor's parents showed up at the scene, he thought his father was Satan. Trevor took off his shirt, crossed two of the knives over his chest, and impaled himself through the heart.

❧

In the mid-1970s, Fouad Talabani of Munich, Germany, became very upset when he found out that his father-in-law had been a Nazi doctor in a German concentration camp. So he stabbed his wife, Freya, to death.

❧

Juan Miguel Alvarez was heartbroken when his marriage ended in 2005. So he drove his Jeep Grand Cherokee to the Metrolink railroad tracks in Glendale, California, and waited for the next train to end it all for him. When he saw the southbound train approaching, he chickened out and fled the car. The train crashed into the SUV, derailed, crashed into a parked train, and hit a northbound commuter train. At least 11 passengers were killed and 180 were injured in the crash. Juan survived without a scratch.

Facing murder charges related to the deaths of those passengers, Juan once again sought the easy way out. He went to a friend's house, where he cut his wrists and stabbed himself in the chest. The friend called 911. Juan was saved from death for the second time that night.

There was one more chance for Juan to get his death wish: Prosecutors were hoping he would get the death penalty. Once again, Juan was saved. The man who killed eleven people when he failed twice to kill himself was convicted of murder in 2008 and sentenced to eleven consecutive life terms.

ex

Stephen Milburn was a divorced, forty-three-year-old, frequently drunk, out-of-work actor from Coxhoe, England, who often complained that people harassed him but whose neighbors complained that it was he who harassed them. He had spent some time in prison for threatening a neighbor with a toy gun.

When his decomposing corpse was found on the kitchen floor of his home in November 2004, police launched a massive murder investigation that lasted ten months and involved more than thirty officers, a team of forensic experts, and two autopsies. Police also went to unusual extremes to remind the people of Coxhoe that Stephen was not a pedophile, as if it mattered one way or the other, now that he was dead.

At the end of the investigation, coroner Andrew Tweddle ruled that Stephen's death was not a homicide. There was one small nick below the neck (perhaps indicating a false start), but it was the two gigantic self-inflicted stab wounds to the chest with his own kitchen knife that killed him.

❧

On July 15, 1987, neighbors of twenty-six-year-old Sharon Araoye called police to the Riverdale Hills section of Washington, D.C., because Sharon was doing strange things to herself. Police found a bleeding man leaning against a car in front of her apartment. He pointed to Sharon's apartment and told them that they had been smoking "loveboat" marijuana laced with the hallucinogen PCP, and that she had gone crazy and stabbed him several times.

Sharon was running around naked inside her apartment, ranting incoherently about Satan and Jehovah, waving a book she had clutched in one hand, and savagely attacking herself with a butcher's knife in the other. She stabbed herself repeatedly in the torso, groin, and eye. When she ran outside and advanced menacingly on the large group of spectators who had gathered to watch, police shot her. Incredibly, she lived another five hours.

❧

Jennifer Cruise, a forty-four-year-old nurse from Coventry, England, owed her sister £30 (about $50). Unable to come up with the amount herself, she walked over to her neighbor Elaine Wain's house one day in October 2005 and asked if she could borrow the money to pay her sister back. Elaine had lent her money many times before, but this time she refused. So Jennifer stabbed her 130 times.

&

Ethel Matheny, a seventy-one-year-old woman from Ravenswood, West Virginia, made the terrible mistake of opening the door of her trailer home to her neighbor April Yvonne Miller during Easter weekend in 2003. April forced poor Ethel to write her a check for $5,000 because her boyfriend needed to get his truck fixed. April then stabbed Ethel in the neck with a pair of scissors, choked her with a telephone cord, and set Ethel's trailer on fire. Upon returning home, April stabbed herself a little bit, then set fire to her own trailer in an effort to confuse the police.

April is now serving a life sentence at the Lakin Correctional Center in West Virginia. She is looking for pen pals, preferably nice Christian folk.

&

Swedish foreign minister Anna Lindh went clothes shopping with a friend on the same September day in 2003 and in the same department store where Mijailo Mijailovic decided to wander around for a while. Mijailo had no intention of buying anything that day. He just went from department to department, inspecting merchandise, and listening to the voices in his head. One of those, he said, was the voice of Jesus.

Mijailo had no money in his pockets, but he did have a knife. When the voices told him to follow Anna, he did. And when they told him to stab her repeatedly in the arms and chest, he did.

Anna died the following day. Mijailo told police he had no idea at the time that the woman he had killed was Anna Lindh. He had no interest in politics, no plan, no personal agenda. He was just doing what he was told, like when he stabbed his father repeatedly in the back in 1996 (Dad survived).

🐾

The first thing twenty-six-year-old Tiffany Keeny noticed when she woke up one morning in 2004 was that she was sitting in a hot tub somewhere in Spencer, West Virginia. She had apparently passed out after a night of drugging and boozing with her boyfriend, Benjamin Murray, and their mutual friend, Cristal Coon.

The second thing she noticed was that Ben was in the hot tub with her. The third thing she noticed was that Ben was dead. He had passed out and drowned right next to her in the Jacuzzi.

⌘

Mary Parnell, a seventy-nine-year-old grandmother from North Carolina, was going about her day just minding her own business when young Larry Whitfield broke into her house. Earlier that day in September 2008, Larry had tried to rob a bank, but that hadn't quite worked out the way he'd planned. He took off looking for a place to hide, and found it in Mary's house. Although Larry never touched her, he scared her so badly when he burst into her home that she died of a heart attack brought on by pure fright. Larry will spend the rest of his life in jail, mostly for being both stupid and unlucky. Prosecutors could not charge him with bank robbery or with murder, but they did successfully argue that the bumbling twenty-one-year-old was guilty of kidnapping.

⌘

Augusta Gein lived on a lonely farm in Wisconsin with her devoted son, Edward. Their quiet lives together might have seemed unremarkable to the casual observer (if there had been one), but things really started to get weird when Augusta died in the mid-1950s.

Ed missed his mother terribly and was utterly unable to live without her. So about a year after Mom passed away, he dug her up from the graveyard and brought her back home.

Twelve months in the ground hadn't done much for whatever physical charms Augusta might have had in life, but Ed came up with a really great idea. Every now and then, in the dead of night, he would sneak into the cemetery and dig up a fresh female corpse. He used the various body parts to reconstruct his mother.

Then Ed had a whole bunch of other really great ideas. He started bringing home corpses, not just to keep dear old Mom in fresh limbs and skin, but he kept some of the bodies whole and arranged them around her to keep her company. He also discovered a knack for making furniture, clothing, and home accessories. He had an armchair made from actual arms.

Ed was so happy to have found a way out of loneliness that his appetite was better than ever. He was especially fond of his own personal recipe for a stew made from human hearts.

Ed Gein was the real-life inspiration for countless horror movie characters, among them Norman Bates (*Psycho*), Leatherface (*The Texas Chainsaw Massacre*), and Jame Gumb and Hannibal Lecter (*Silence of the Lambs*). Yet, his own story is so gory and his pathology so disturbing that Hollywood has never quite found a true-to-life way of bringing the tale to the silver screen. Ed was a thousand times worse than any monster ever conceived in the dark hearts of even the most depraved horror movie screenwriters.

Ed died quietly at the age of seventy-seven in a hospital for the criminally insane in 1984.

Mark Fidrych, nicknamed "The Bird" for his curly-haired resemblance to *Sesame Street*'s Big Bird, was a much-loved pitcher for the 1976 Detroit Tigers. He was skinny and funny-looking, and utterly disarming. He was praised as much for his athletic ability as for his charming habit of whispering to the baseball before hurling it. He also drove his opponents crazy when he stopped to fuss over and groom the pitcher's mound. A series of injuries cut short an otherwise promising career in the major leagues.

In April 2009, while he was doing some repairs underneath the ten-wheel dump truck he drove for his construction business, his clothes became entangled in the power takeoff shaft. The shaft began spinning and strangled The Bird in his own shirt.

"The Ballad of the Green Berets" was written by a Vietnam-era combat medic named Barry Sadler. He often said that the words to the famous song came to him after a night of debauchery at a Mexican whorehouse.

When his Army days were behind him, it became more and more apparent that his musical legacy would probably never rise above the level of one-hit wonder. Sadler went on to live hard, recklessly and without fear, all the rest of his days. His legacy rivaled that of Paul Bunyan.

It was said that someone once slashed him across the stomach with a carpet knife in a Nashville bar and that Sadler refused to go to the hospital. Instead he had a few more whiskeys, then went home and sewed himself up.

While living in Guatemala in 1988, Sadler was shot in the head. Some accounts say the gunman was one of the contra rebels Sadler was training to fight the communist Sandinistas of Nicaragua. Others insist he was shot by a burglar who broke into his home, a place Sadler had dubbed Rancho Borracho (Drunken Ranch). Still others say he was shot by a mugger while getting into a taxi. Either way, two things are certain: Sadler's shooter was never caught, and getting shot in the head didn't kill him.

The extraordinary Barry Sadler died a rather ordinary death. He passed away of heart failure in Tennessee in 1989.

Joseph Plastino Jr. of New Providence, Pennsylvania, was driving home late one night in June 2006. The last thing he saw as his Jeep Comanche pickup truck came around a slight bend on Truce Road was the two thousand–pound Belgian workhorse standing dead center in his lane, looking him right in the eye.

The horse was as smart as it was massive. It had managed to work open the gate at the edge of the farm where it lived and escaped into the night.

It's impossible to know with any certainty whether Plastino would have survived the crash if he had been wearing his seat belt. Both the man and his truck were a crumpled heap after hitting the horse, skidding onto the other side of the road, crashing through a fence, rolling *up* an embankment, destroying a windmill, and stopping only when the truck hit the concrete porch of a house two hundred feet away.

The horse was still alive when police arrived at the scene.

Derek Omand Brown, a former cab driver from Edinburgh, Scotland, developed a strange habit late in his life. He liked to eat discarded latex gloves.

Described as a hardworking man with a Calvinistic work ethic, he became distraught when he was diagnosed with a wasting disease that left him unable to keep his job. He eventually agreed to move into a nursing home in Wales, where his brother lived close by.

Derek had been warned by the medical staff the first time he threw up and the nurses found three gloves. They told him that this compulsion to eat medical supplies straight out of the wastebaskets could prove very harmful. Derek was always remorseful and always promised to stop, but the urge was overpowering. He once ate ten rubber gloves and a bunch of cotton swabs. On another occasion, he required surgery to remove a variety of foreign objects from his gastric system.

Derek's odd compulsions finally killed him in February 2008. During the autopsy, the coroner found two more rubber gloves in Derek's small intestine. He was sixty-four.

Relatives of twenty-year-old Laboni Begum of Bangladesh were understandably heartbroken at the news of her premature death in May 2009. Twelve family members piled into a small bus driven by a trusted friend and made the trek to the Dhaka Medical College Hospital to retrieve Laboni's body for burial in their hometown of Basail Upazila. On the way home, the bus crashed into a pickup truck, killing five more members of the family.

🐛

When John Kelly of Somerville, Massachusetts, died in 1991, his wife, Geraldine, didn't have the heart to tell their children the truth behind his demise. She told them instead that their drunken father had been run over by a car in Las Vegas.

At the age of fifty-four, as Geraldine lay on her own death-bed in November 2004, she finally came clean. She told her grown children that she had shot John in the head in 1991, then stuffed him into two garbage bags, put the bags in a six-by-three-foot freezer, sealed the freezer with duct tape, put a lock on the freezer door, and had the freezer shipped to the Planet Self Storage. Police found John Kelly's remains exactly where Geraldine said they would be.

🐛

W. Delight Malitsky of Indiana, Pennsylvania, had undergone treatment for a liver ailment at UPMC Presbyterian Hospital in the fall of 2001. A few months later, the seventy-seven-year-old woman, now well enough to live at home, decided to separate from her husband, seventy-year-old Andrii Malyc-kyi. She moved in with her daughter who lived in Philadelphia.

When Malitsky passed away in February 2002, her estranged husband stepped in to handle the disposition of the body. He rented a van and convinced an employee of the John R. Freed Funeral Home to release the body. He packed her in dry ice and drove three hundred miles across the state, back to UPMC Presbyterian Hospital in Pittsburgh. Malyc-kyi told a security guard that he had been so pleased with the way the hospital had treated his wife the previous year that he decided to donate her body to the facility for scientific research.

When authorities ascertained that no foul play had taken place, they returned the body to Malitsky's daughter, who immediately arranged for her mother's cremation.

Joyce Germain, a fifty-nine-year-old American living in Sydney, Australia, was reported missing in April 2006. When police entered her home, they found her on the bathroom floor. She had been dead about a week.

Her dress was pulled up to her neck. Her vagina was partially shaved and clasped shut with a clothespin. A construction hat and a foot spa were balanced on her torso. A toaster was dangling from the shower curtain rod, and the electrical cord of her iron was wrapped around her neck. On the floor near her body, there was a knife, a disposable razor, and a used hypodermic needle. Police believe she may have died of natural causes.

&

Milton Taylor lived on a houseboat on Australia's Gold Coast. He was still mourning the death of his longtime companion, who had committed suicide a few months before.

In January 2008, he discovered a complete stranger lying unconscious in his bed. The stranger turned out to be a woman named Dawn Sword, who had taken an overdose of pills in an attempt to take her own life.

Milton became enraged at the sight. He grabbed a sixteen-inch fiberglass pole and began beating the unconscious woman. When that didn't wake her up, he started yelling obscenities at her and smashed a ceramic coffee mug into her face so hard that fragments of the cup became lodged in her cheekbones and knocked her teeth out. That didn't wake her up, either.

Milton finally calmed down enough to call the police. He told them that he had discovered an intruder.

Milton was not charged with murder. The coroner ruled that Dawn was already dying on her own. The assault on the dead and/or dying woman was nonetheless brutal, but the courts had no idea how to deal with this situation. There was no legal precedent or similar incident in Australia's history.

꙰

Brian Williams, a fifty-three-year-old professor of criminology from Sheffield, England, was driving home from a Guide Girls (Girl Scouts) center where his wife, Suzanne, was a troop leader. It was a dark night in March 2007, the air was full of a frosty mist, the area was poorly lit, and it was close to midnight as he drove toward the entrance gate of the facility. It's also entirely possible that Williams's windshield wasn't fully defrosted as he drove away, making the conditions exactly right for what happened next.

As the professor drove through the low stone wall upon which the four-foot iron gate was mounted, the wooden beam used to keep the gate closed crashed through the windshield and the rear window. Unfortunately, it didn't keep going. It pinned the professor underneath it. And then the rest of the gate fell on his Renault.

This may be the only known case of a person simultaneously trapped in his car by a wooden beam and smothered to death by a gate.

In 2007, Jordi Giro bought a foreclosed home at auction from a bank in Madrid. When he arrived to inspect his new property, he found the mummified corpse of the previous owner sitting on the living room sofa.

The salty air of the seaside town of Roses had kept the body of the fifty-ish woman from rotting outright. It is very likely that there was some kind of smell, but the area is mostly occupied by tourists and short-term vacationers. The few permanent residents of the surrounding neighborhood are well known for their penchant for minding their own business.

Based on the date of the woman's last mortgage payment, the bank estimated she had been dead for six years.

In October 2007, a squirrel bit through a power line in Bayonne, New Jersey, and fell in a flaming ball onto a Toyota Camry belonging to Lindsey Millar. The car blew up. The only reported fatality was that of the squirrel.

❧

In November 2007, police in Manchester, England, found a body that matched the description of a thirty-seven-year-old missing man. Gina Partington was notified immediately that her missing son, Thomas Dennison, had, unfortunately, been found dead. Gina went to the morgue and positively identified the body as that of her son, and went about the sad business of arranging a funeral and cremation.

She wailed and wept as any mother would have done. Four days later, Tommy showed up, perfectly alive. He had gone to spend a little quiet time in the great outdoors, he said.

Manchester police now say they have a pretty good idea of the identity of the mistakenly cremated corpse, but wanted to be sure before they made any more public announcements.

❧

Hans Steininger of Austria was famous for having the world's longest beard. Some accounts state that the beard measured four and a half feet, while others claim it was as much as eight feet long.

In 1567, there was an enormous fire in Steininger's home-town of Braunau. As he fled down the stairs of his house to escape the blaze, he got tangled up in his own whiskers, fell, and broke his neck. He died instantly.

🦎

Kevin McKeon from Somerset, England, was pretty drunk the night in August 2003 when his cell phone's battery fell into a sewer. Still, the spry young man thought this was one of those problems any idiot could solve. So he removed the sewer grate and kneeled to look for the lost object.

Sometime later, Jamie Passmore walked by and saw a pair of sneakers sticking out of the sewer. At first Jamie thought someone had put the shoes on a couple of broomsticks as a joke, but soon discovered that the rest of Kevin was still attached to the sneakers. Unable to lift himself back out onto the street, Kevin had drowned in sewer sludge.

🦎

Tammy Lewis and Magdeline Alvina Middlesworth were members of the Order of the Divine Will, a religion invented by Alan Bushey. The elderly Magdeline gave all of her money to support the congregation, which had a total of six members. It is not clear whether that number included Rev. Bushey and Lewis's two young children. Lewis took Middlesworth into her home in Necedah, Wisconsin, cared for her, and served as her power of attorney.

When Middlesworth died at the age of ninety, Rev. Bushey convinced Lewis to prop her corpse up on the toilet and wait for God to resurrect her. It was all in the power of prayer, he said. In the meantime, they should continue to deposit Middlesworth's monthly Social Security and retirement annuity checks to support the church, as the old lady had done for the past few years.

Sheriff's deputies were sent to the Lewis residence on May 7, 2008, after Bernice Metz called to tell them that she had been unable to get in touch with her ninety-year-old sister for several weeks. At first Lewis resisted, but eventually let them inside. The house reeked of incense, burning wood, and rotting corpse. The lump of decay on the toilet was identified as Middlesworth.

Lewis's teenage son explained to detectives that, according to Rev. Bushey, demons were destroying Middlesworth's appearance to convince them that she would not rise from the dead.

FUN FACTS ABOUT DEATH

So what in the world is "fun" about death, you may ask. I suppose it's fair to say that only the most twisted of all human beings would put those two words together in the same sentence. And here we are, you and I.

What's fun is the contemplation of little details we try not to discuss in polite company, which become irresistible in the quietest moments or with the right kindred soul. So many questions emerge when you give yourself permission to think about the unthinkable: Exactly what happens to all those urns filled with ashes after a couple of generations? Do the descendants mistake them for vases, rinse them out, and stick some flowers in them? Or, if not vases, might they be used—ick—as cookie jars? Can you imagine having your urn and ashes inadvertently sold at a yard sale for a couple of bucks by your great-great-granddaughter-in-law, or surrendered to a pawn shop for the price of a bucket of chicken? I can.

It's this kind of imagining—not to mention the search for the real answers—that I find endlessly fascinating and, yes, most definitely fun.

More people die of natural causes in January than in any other month of the year. The mortality rate tends to be at its lowest in August, so that's when most morticians go on vacation.

The top five causes of non-illness-related death, in order, are: (1) traveling, especially by plane, train, and automobile, (2) poisoning, (3) drug overdose, (4) falling down, and (5) drowning.

Defibrillators—those ubiquitous electric "paddles" most often used in movies and on television to bring the dead back to life—are of no use whatsoever when a real-life patient has flat-lined. The device is designed to stabilize a fluttery heart, not a dead-stopped one.

Many passengers of the ill-fated *Titanic* fared no better in death than they did in life. While the bodies of first-class passengers were placed in coffins, second-class and "steerage" passengers were put into canvas bags. Crew members were put on ice in the cargo hold. Those who could not be identified or classified in any particular way—almost one in three of the dead—were buried at sea, which is to say they were just left in the water.

The first people to whip themselves bloody in a ritualistic way (as opposed to doing so in a kinky, sexual kind of way) are believed to be the survivors of the bubonic plague. The plague killed off nearly a third of all Europeans in a two-year period in the Middle Ages (1348–1350). Florence, Italy, was especially hard-hit; nearly four out of five people in that city died of the plague. Many of the survivors, believing the disease was divine punishment for their sins, thought they might be able to get back in God's good graces through self-flagellation. A whole bunch of them died anyway. The rest were scarred for life.

Today, bubonic plague is easily treatable with a round of antibiotics.

🐛

We have the ancient Greeks to thank for the image of the Grim Reaper as a towering, fearsome figure wielding a scythe in one bony hand and an hourglass in the other. As the story goes, Kronos was the son of the gods Uranus and Gaia. Uranus was something of a paranoid maniac who forced his children back into Gaia's womb because he feared they were plotting against him. Unbeknownst to Uranus, Gaia had given a scythe to Kronos just before he went in. Kronos escaped by using the scythe to cut through his mother's belly. He then used it to castrate Uranus.

Kronos later married his sister and together they had many children. Like his father, Kronos feared that his children would someday overtake him. So he swallowed them whole, one by one, as they soon were born.

🐛

There is a sect of Mexican Catholics who worship the Grim Reaper as a saint. They call her (yes, her) "Santa Muerte" (Saint Death).

The image of this saint is familiar to us all—a skeletal figure in a hooded robe with a scythe—but instead of holding an hourglass in one hand, she carries a small globe of the world, representing dominion over Earth. Dangling from a belt around her waist, she also carries the scales of justice.

There are shrines to Santa Muerte all over Mexico, even in shop windows, churches, and chapels. Worshippers ask the saint for protection from evildoers or assistance in punishing their enemies. These are typically the sorts of favors that would horrify real saints.

Much to the chagrin of this devout group, the Catholic Church has repeatedly refused to grant them official recognition.

Some Buddhist monks believe that to separate completely from this life and achieve total enlightenment, a person must mummify himself. They estimate that it takes about two thousand days to accomplish this feat.

Successful mummification requires the body to be completely without fat or moisture. In the first thousand days, the monk eats nothing but seeds and nuts to rid the body of all fatty matter. The next thousand days is a "drying out" period. Considering that human beings are made up of about 80 percent water, this is one of the trickiest—not to mention most painful—aspects of the process. During this period, the only things the monk ingests are pine bark and roots, and a tea made from the sap of the urushi tree, which causes uncontrollable vomiting and diarrhea. If the monk survives this period, he is sealed up in a stone chamber just big enough to allow him to sit in the lotus position while he waits for death to finally put an end to his suffering.

After an appropriate stretch of time, people will peer into the chamber to see if the mummification worked. It hardly ever does. After all that agony, most monks just die a horrible death and are, presumably, forced to come back and do it all over again through the process of reincarnation.

Bodies that are buried in warm, moist places often become too acidic for putrefaction to occur properly. The body fat turns into a waxy, greasy substance that smells like ammonia and cheese and produces a faint yellow flame when lit.

By contrast, a body that is cremated burns in many brilliant colors as the flames consume the flesh and its various salts and chemicals down to the bones. Obese corpses burn much more easily and colorfully than skinny ones.

You are more likely to be killed by a champagne cork than by a poisonous spider.

Robert Todd Lincoln, the oldest son of Abraham Lincoln and the only one of his children to reach adulthood, was present at or in the vicinity of the assassinations of three presidents: his father's, President Garfield's, and President McKinley's. After the last one, he refused to attend any more public functions.

In ancient Rome, the oldest surviving male member of the family was required to inhale the last breath of a dying relative.

Some caskets are now available with innerspring mattresses and adjustable headrests.

The fastest-growing segment of the death-related market is funerals for pets. Most caskets fall in the $200 to $300 range. Many pet cremation facilities offer chapels for religious rites and can organize solemn graveside services for the feathery or furry departed.

In most states, you are not obligated to buy a casket from a funeral parlor or mortician. You can be buried in your grandmother's hope chest if you like.

About 200,000 people die every year in the United States as a direct result of medical errors. That's six times more than the number of people who kill themselves on purpose.

In America, burials deposit more than 800,000 gallons of embalming fluid into the soil each year. Cremation pumps dioxins, hydrochloric acid, sulfur dioxide, and carbon dioxide into the air. The only truly eco-friendly way to dispose of a body may be to let an endangered species eat it.

Newspaper obituary pages were the precursor to modern-day celebrity magazines and gossip columns. Prior to the 1700s, there was no such thing as a celebrity in the way we currently think of them, and only the lives and deaths of monarchs, religious leaders, and other "important" people made the news.

However, when newspaper publishers realized that people actually enjoyed reading the death notices—especially if the obituaries were filled with scandal, gossip, and other titillating details—they expanded the definition of "important" to include the odd, the eccentric, and the probably insane. In turn, those who suffered an irresistible craving for the limelight began cultivating their eccentricities in ever more elaborate and public ways. The belief was that their antics would help them amass enough of a reputation among the locals, which would make them worthy of a memorable obituary. This in turn would legitimize their status as a "celebrated" citizen (albeit a dead one).

Paris Hilton, it turns out, is not a modern invention.

A person is 33,000 times more likely to die from mistakes made in the hospital than in an airplane crash.

Many European countries reuse graves, a legacy of the two-hundred-year-old Napoleonic Code. Much to the horror and indignation of many a proper British citizen, England is considering changing its laws to allow graves to be reused up to six times. The country is running out of room in which to bury its dead, and throwing bodies into the ocean is not a dignified alternative. Also, no one wants to give up what little real estate is left for those who are not still alive and kicking.

In America, where there is much more land and people believe that living forever is a matter of ingesting sufficient amounts of organic fiber, no such laws are likely to be enacted anytime soon.

Some years ago, cemetery developers in Germany made the terrible mistake of purchasing land whose soil was mostly clay. As a result, bodies buried in such locations do not decompose. High moisture levels and low temperatures cause dead bodies to turn into hard, pasty-gray, waxlike mummies. This has caused a huge problem for gravediggers trying to reuse older plots. "When you hit them with the spade," they say, "the bodies sound kind of hollow."

For a time, some of Britain's notoriously sensationalistic newspapers relished pointing out whenever the number 666 appeared on the license plates of cars involved in deadly accidents. Tired of catering to the fears of superstitious citizens and the tabloids' lust for the macabre, the British government stopped issuing license plates containing the evil number in 1991. No word on whether they'll do the same for the number 13.

As the wide-open spaces of America become less plentiful, murderers have found more convenient ways of disposing of their victims. At any given time, there are hundreds of rotting corpses waiting to become grisly discoveries in the nation's thirteen million self-storage warehouses.

Compared to the United States, India has to pack three times as many people into one-third of the geographic space. The competition for real estate and elbow room is, therefore, quite stiff.

Cemeteries are often used for dual purposes. Some serve as tearooms and vending stalls, where the graves conveniently double as sitting benches and display shelves. Cemeteries are also popular tent sites for newcomers and squatters.

It helps that Indian literature has no relationship to horror fiction as Americans know it, so a fear of ghosts among Indians is practically nonexistent.

🐛

Schools that teach funerary sciences these days must also include special training regarding the customs of a wide variety of ethnic, cultural, and religious groups. Trimming the beard of a Muslim corpse, for example, could prove disastrous.

🐛

Many morticians are happy to accommodate the last wishes of a nudist and will prepare the body to be buried or cremated naked. In most cases, however, the funeral is a closed-casket affair, but only out of consideration for the nudist's "textiled" relatives.

If the deceased and/or his family insists on an open casket, the mortician may arrange the body in such a way that the bottom half of the coffin covers the region below the belly button.

🐛

About 90 percent of nudists are buried with their clothes on.

People from various parts of Central America celebrate El Día de los Muertos, or the Day of the Dead. The tradition was begun by ancient Mesoamerican cultures that long preceded the invasion of the Spanish conquistadors. Missionaries folded the "pagan" rites into one of the established Catholic holidays as a way of gently cajoling the native peoples to accept Catholicism, and killed the ones who refused to convert. This is why Día de los Muertos begins on Halloween and lasts through All Saints and All Souls Day.

People honor their ancestors by setting up altars in their homes, or arranging to spend these three days in the cemetery with their dearly departed. The required artifacts include a doughnut-shaped bread, symbolizing the cycle of life and death and the nourishment of the soul, and candles to light the way for the spirits to find their still-living relatives. Toys also figure prominently, as a way to show fearlessness in the face of death.

In Ghana, the dead are commonly buried in caskets that symbolize the way they lived, their professions, or something about their personalities.

A sculptor named Seth Kane Kwe is the country's most acclaimed personalized coffin craftsman. For a politician or other powerful member of the community, for example, Kane (pronounced *Kahn-nee)* has sculpted coffins in the shape of a leopard. For a mother who is protective of her kids, a coffin in the shape of a chicken is a popular choice.

One of Kane's coffins can cost as much as an average Ghanaian's annual income. Members of the family, friends, and neighbors will often pool their resources to ensure that a recently departed member of their community is sent to the next life in style.

A female hyena's clitoris can become so large and rigid when it is engorged that it can crush her offspring's head to death as it exits the birth canal.

Funeral planners are becoming as popular as wedding planners, especially for people whose tastes run from the extravagant to the eccentric. One of the first of these businesses was established in Scotland by Barbara Faro and Esther Aronsfeld. Their company is called Funerals to Die For.

According to Centennial Park, a funeral services provider in Australia, some of the most popular funeral songs include the following:

- "Danny Boy" (various artists)

- "Ding Dong the Witch Is Dead" (from *The Wizard of Oz*, sung by Munchkins)

- "My Way" (Frank Sinatra)

- "Always Look on the Bright Side of Life" (Monty Python)

- "The Show Must Go On" (Queen)

- "Wonderful World" (Louis Armstrong)

- "I'll Sleep When I'm Dead" (Bon Jovi)

- "Time to Say Goodbye" (Andrea Bocelli and Sarah Brightman)

- "Another One Bites the Dust" (Queen)

Once or twice a year, the New York City Metropolitan Transit Authority discovers that a sleeping passenger on the bus or train is actually a dead person. In every instance, hundreds of passengers come and go, sitting or standing next to the expired rider, and never even notice.

❧

About 30 percent of people choose cremation because it's cheaper than burial. About 3 percent choose it because they don't want bugs eating their bodies. An additional 2 percent state "claustrophobia" as the reason.

❧

In 1975, only 6 percent of Americans chose cremation (or had it chosen for them) as the means of final disposition of their mortal remains. By 2005, that number had risen to 39 percent. The Cremation Association of North America estimates that by 2025 more than 57 percent of Americans will be cremated.

Canada has already reached that number. In the United Kingdom, more than 72 percent of their dead were cremated in 2005.

❧

In Hawaii, 66 percent of all corpses are cremated; in Alabama, only 9 percent.

With the significant rise in popularity of cremation over burial in recent years, funeral parlors and cemeteries have had to resort to creative ways of generating revenue. Many now offer their lovely grounds, chapels, mausoleums, and large gathering rooms for weddings, bar mitzvahs, and family reunions.

As people become ever more reluctant to view death as a mournful experience, alternatives to traditional funerals and the final disposition of the body are gaining popularity. Some examples include the following:

- Ashes can be incorporated into a work of art. There are artists who "paint" the ashes directly into the canvas to create a portrait of the deceased or a landscape of his favorite vacation spot.

- The hollowed-out horns of animals the deceased may have killed could be the ideal receptacle for a hunter's cremains.

- Funerary jewelry allows many members of the family to carry or wear a deceased loved one's cremains.

- A gigantic columbarium allows an entire family's ashes to mingle and spend the rest of eternity together.

In the Tanatoraga region of Sulawesi in Indonesia, family members keep the dead bodies of their loved ones at home while they make funeral arrangements. The ceremonies often take several days to organize. In the meantime, the dead person is treated like a slightly incapacitated living person. The corpse is seated at the table during mealtimes and tucked into bed at night.

Only nine of the fifty states have no specific laws banning necrophilia (the practice of having sex with a corpse). However, other criminal charges may apply.

Amusement parks are pretty safe places for people to have fun. Generally, only two or three people die from roller-coaster accidents every year. Most others are only injured, or stranded upside-down for a few hours.

Proponents of the Taser stun gun argue that it is a safe and effective way of disabling a potentially dangerous criminal. Since 2001, almost five hundred people have been accidentally killed by the fifty thousand–volt hits.

You are 233 times more likely to die riding a bicycle—with or without a helmet—anywhere in America than you are riding a violently scary ride in any amusement park.

To "die peacefully after a long illness" very often requires an unusually large dose of morphine.

In America, celebrities die at an average rate of 148.6 per year.[*] For a while, it appeared that 2009 would go down in history as

---

[*] It is perhaps more accurate to say, "celebrities known to most Americans." As a group, we tend to be woefully (sometimes willfully) unaware that there are famous people in other parts of the world.

a particularly deadly year for famous people. Interestingly, that was just an illusion.

The total number of dead celebrities barely broke one hundred by the end of 2009. What made it seem so much worse was that the overwhelming majority of them died in an enormous clump during the spring and summer months.

Depending upon the sharpness of the blade, the skill of the executioner, and the doggedness of the victim's will to live, the human head can remain fully conscious for fifteen seconds or longer after decapitation.

On average, right-handed people live about a decade longer than southpaws. One contributing factor may be that about 2,500 lefties are killed every year by tools and implements designed for right-handed people. Power saws are particularly deadly to lefties.

At room temperature, the average corpse cools at a rate of one or two degrees per hour. Skinny corpses go cold much faster.

Until the 1800s, there was no such thing as a funeral director. When someone died, family members typically hired a furniture maker to build a casket. Little by little, the furniture makers took on more of the responsibilities of caring for the dead. Eventually a more specialized profession was born.

Not all corpses undergo rigor mortis. Those that do can remain in that state for up to three days. After that they start to relax again, as muscle and tissue begin to decompose.

You are more likely to drown in your own bathtub than in a public swimming pool.

The ancient Hindu practice of *sati* (meaning "faithful wife" and often pronounced in English as "suttee") was a ritual in which the favorite spouse of a recently departed man would hurl herself into his funeral pyre to ensure an eternal union in the afterlife. The rite was also said to expiate the sins of both the husband and his wife.

As the centuries passed, the meaning and the practice underwent a series of variations. It is believed that with the evolution of cultural mores and greater enlightenment, widowhood came to be seen as sinful, so most wives were thrown into the fire by force.

The practice was banned in 1829 under British rule, but the problem of the occasional self-immolating widow still pops up from time to time.

About one hundred people die every year from choking on their ballpoint pens.

The United States was the first country in the world to institute the practice of executing criminals by lethal injection. Twenty years later, China became the second.

The first death row inmate to die in this manner was Charles Brooks, who was executed in 1982 in the great state of Texas. The thousandth prisoner was Marvallous Keene, whose sentence was carried out in July 2009 in Ohio.

🐛

The Nazis invented lethal injection.

🐛

The exact time of death listed on a death certificate is, at best, a pretty good guess. Even when the deceased expires in the presence of medical professionals and other witnesses, there is not likely to be a "moment of death." Death is a process that occurs in phases, with different organs shutting down at their own pace. At a bedside vigil, for example, loved ones may think the moment occurs when the person stops breathing and his eyes go blank. In fact, that person is capable of experiencing several more moments of mental life after the heart has stopped beating, the final "death rattle" has been uttered, and the occasional last bit of flatulent fanfare has erupted.

The practice of closing or sealing a corpse's eyes as soon after death as possible arose from a variety of superstitions. Besides the fact that having a corpse staring straight at you can be rather unnerving, it was once believed that a corpse whose eyes refused to close was an omen presaging more deaths. Closing the eyes was a way of keeping the Reaper at bay.

Ancient Egyptians were as devoted to their household pets as modern man. When a beloved cat died, the owners shaved off their eyebrows. If the dearly departed pet was a dog, the owners would shave off all their body hair, including the hair on their heads.

It was once legal for a dead person to "grant" consent by signing a legal document if someone guided the corpse's hand while the body was still warm.

The use of white satin as the traditional lining of a coffin is believed to have originated from a sermon John Donne wrote in 1630, days before his own death. Specifically, the line that inspired the tradition was "just as the body is shrouded in white linen, [so] may be the soul."

Sources

AAP General News (Australia)

Agence France-Presse

Akron Beacon Journal

AM New York

Amnesty International

AOL News

AP Worldstream

Asbury Park Press (Monmouth County, New Jersey)

AsiaOne News

Associated Press

Bay City News (San Francisco)

BBC News

Belfast Telegraph (Ireland)

Bergen County Record (New Jersey)

Birmingham Post (England)

Blakemore, Colin, and Sheila Jennett. *The Oxford Companion to the Body*. Oxford, England: Oxford University Press, 2002.

Bondi, Victor. *American Decades: 1940-1949*. Detroit: Gale Research, 1995.

Boston Globe

Boston Herald

Bowker, John. *The Concise Oxford Dictionary of World Religions.* Oxford: Oxford University Press, 2000.

Brandon Sun (Canada)

Business Wire

California Missions Resource Center

Cape Times (South Africa)

CBS News

Charleston Daily Mail (West Virginia)

Charleston Gazette (West Virginia)

Chicago Sun-Times

Chicago Tribune

CNN

Cotterell, Arthur. *A Dictionary of World Mythology.* Oxford: Oxford University Press, 1997.

Coventry Evening Telegraph (England)

Cremation Association of North America

Croatian Times (Kent, England)

Daily Mail (London)

Daily News (Los Angeles)

Daily News Egypt (Giza)

Daily Post (Liverpool, England)

Daily Record (Glasgow, Scotland)

Dayton Daily News (Dayton, Ohio)

Death Penalty Information Center

The Denver Channel (ABC News affiliate)

Der Spiegel (Germany)

Deseret News (Salt Lake City, Utah)

Encyclopaedia Britannica

Entertainment Weekly

ESPN

Evening Chronicle (Newcastle, England)

Evening Standard (London, England)

Evening Times (Scotland)

Extra (celebrity newsmagazine)

Football Digest

Hindustan Times (New Delhi, India)

Huffington Post

Independent (London)

Insider

Irish Independent (Dublin)

Journal (Newcastle, England)

Kastenbaum, Robert. *Macmillan Encyclopedia of Death and Dying*. New York: Macmillan Reference USA, 2002.

Knight Ridder/Tribune News Service

Lancaster New Era (Lancaster, Pennsylvania)

Las Vegas Sun

Lighthouse Depot/Lighthouse Digest (Wells, Maine)

Los Angeles Times

Major League Baseball News

Matlock Mercury (Matlock, England)

Melton, J. Gordon. *Encyclopedia of Occultism & Parapsychology.*
  Detroit: Gale Group, 2001.

Miami Herald

Milwaukee Journal Sentinel

Mirror (London)

MSNBC News

National Museum of Funeral History

Nederland, Colorado, Chamber of Commerce

New Straits Times (Singapore)

New York Times

News-Sun (Waukegan, Illinois)

Newsday (Long Island, New York)

Newsweek

Northern Echo (Durham, England)

Orlando Sentinel

People (London, England)

Peterkin, Allan D. *One Thousand Beards: A Cultural History of
  Facial Hair*. Vancouver: Arsenal Pulp, 2001.

Portland Press Herald (Portland, Maine)

Post Tribune (Indiana)

Press (New Zealand)

Press and Journal (Aberdeen, Scotland)

Proceso (Mexico City)

Quadrant (Australia)

Racing Post (London)

Ramsland, Katherine M. *Cemetery Stories: Haunted Graveyards, Embalming Secrets, and the Life of a Corpse after Death.* New York: HarperEntertainment, 2001.

Reuters

Rocky Mountain News (Denver)

Rolling Stone

Scotland on Sunday (Edinburgh)

Scotsman (Edinburgh)

"Six Fun Things You Can Do After You're Dead." Associated Content.com.

South Florida Sun-Sentinel (Fort Lauderdale)

South Wales Echo (Cardiff, Wales)

South Wales Evening Post (Swansea, Wales)

Star (Sheffield, England)

Star Tribune (Minneapolis)

The Straight Dope

Sun (San Bernardino, California)

Sunday Mercury (Birmingham, England)

Sunday Mirror (London)

Sunday Star-Times (Auckland, New Zealand)

Sunday Tribune (South Africa)

Sunderland Echo (Pennywell, England)

Straits Times (Malaysia)

Telegraph Herald (Dubuque, Iowa)

Time

Times West Virginian

Tribune-Review (Pittsburgh)

TV Guide

United News of Bangladesh

United Press International

U.S. National Parks Service

US News & World Report

USA Today

Vanity Fair

Virginian-Pilot (Norfolk, Virginia)

Washington Post (Washington, D.C.)

Washington Times (Washington, D.C.)

Western Daily Press (Bristol, England)

Western Mail (Cardiff, Wales)

Western Morning News (Plymouth, England)

Whittier Daily News (Whittier, California)

Winnipeg Free Press (Canada)

About the Author

Cynthia Ceilán is the author of *Thinning the Herd: Tales of the Weirdly Departed* and *Weirdly Beloved: Tales of Strange Bedfellows, Odd Couplings, and Love Gone Bad*. It only embarrasses her a little to snicker up her sleeve at dead people. She lives in New York City.

www.weirdlyhuman.com